UNIX

First contact

Y. Nishinuma and R. Espesser

Edited by J.A. Mariani,
Department of Computing,
University of Lancaster

**MACMILLAN
EDUCATION**

First published 1987 by
MACMILLAN EDUCATION LTD
Houndmills, Basingstoke, Hampshire RG21 2XS
and London
Companies and representatives throughout the world

Printed in Great Britain by
Camelot Press, Southampton

British Library Cataloguing in Publication Data
Nishinuma, Y.
  UNIX : first contact.---(Macmillan computer science series).
  1. UNIX (Computer operating system)
I. Title II. Espesser, R. III. Mariani, J.A.
  005.4'3   QA76.76.063

ISBN 0-333-43624-5

Contents

Contents

Preface

This book is intended to be an extensive introduction to the UNIX operating system. It consists of 25 sessions which are designed to completed more or less in sequence by the learner at his or her terminal.

Each session has been planned to be covered in about two hours of interactive work. The session should first be read and then the examples keyed in and tried out. A summary of the features covered is included at the end of each session as a revision aid.

Most of the many examples have been tested for this English edition using the Berkeley 4.2 BSD UNIX operating system running on a Digital Equipment Corporation VAX 11-750 with the Bourne Shell.

It is this extensive use of practical examples that should prove most valuable for the newcomer to UNIX. While the examples on your UNIX may not behave exactly as the ones in this book, this should be purely due to 'local variations'.

The book is biased towards the activities of text manipulation (using editors and word processors), the tool-rich UNIX environment and the powerful shell programming facilities. The aim is not to teach languages such as C; it is more to show how, using the shell, such programming can be avoided.

The first six sessions present a 'diagonal' view of UNIX; this should be enough to get you going in terms of logging on, getting familiar with files and directories and started with the editor and word processor. Sessions 7 to 11 introduce more everyday commands that you will often require, including electronic communication with your fellow users.

Sessions 12 to 15 take you further into the capabilities of the UNIX text editor and word processor. The UNIX shell is examined in considerable detail from session 16 onwards. Session 24, which examines the **vi** display oriented, interactive editor, has been added for the English edition.

Appendixes at the end contain summaries of internal commands, special characters and reserved words, together with examples of shell procedures.

Introduction

What is UNIX?

UNIX is the name of an operating system and the utility programs that are supported by it. It was first conceived more than fifteen years ago by researchers at Bell Laboratories. However, with the passage of time, UNIX has become a kind of sociological phenomenon in information technology, spreading to different types of computer. Why this sudden enthusiasm? What is the meaning of UNIX? What does it consist of?

Operating systems

An operating system is a piece of software that controls the operation of a computer. Without it, a computer and its peripherals are no more than mere lumps of machinery.

An operating system must ensure that three functions are carried out, from the user's point of view. First, it must control the link between the CPU and the peripherals. Second, it must analyse the commands that come from the user and react to them. Third, it must manage the files, which are the sole means of storing and retrieving all types of data (programs, text, etc).

For a general purpose computer, it is nowadays usual to find these functions carried out by an interactive, time-shared system (multi-task and multi-user); this was not always the case. In fact, during the 1960s, the majority of computers still worked in 'batch' mode; only one task could be processed by one person at a time. There was no question of being able to interrogate and obtain responses from the machine on the spot (that is, the machines were non-interactive). Pioneering systems, like UNIX, were developed to overcome these disadvantages.

UNIX - Past and present

UNIX originates from 1969, when Ken Thompson developed the first version on Digital Equipment Corporation's PDP minicomputer; a version that was subsequently rewritten in the C language by Dennis Ritchie. Over the years, improvements were made to it, and in 1979 the first commercial version, called UNIX/V7, was produced. This version has since become widespread and is the version upon which the original French edition of this book was based. (In the present English edition, more emphasis has been placed on the Berkeley 4.2 BSD version, see below.) Subsequent versions, System III (1981) and now System V are distributed by AT & T, owner of Bell Laboratories. In addition, as a result of Ken Thompson's period as visiting professor at the University of California, Berkeley (UCB), the organisation Berkeley Software Distribution (BSD) came into being to distribute modified versions of version 7 (for example 4.2 BSD). Since the commercial availability of UNIX/V7, several software houses have created different versions that are either UNIX-based or UNIX-like; some examples are XENIX, UNIPLUS+, UNOS, CROMIX, etc.

What makes UNIX popular?

Currently, the UNIX family is operational on mini, supermini and large machines from various manufacturers. Even Cray, the well known supercomputer, supports a version of UNIX. In the last few years there has been a strong trend towards implementing the system on personal computers, as their power has grown. UNIX is thus the only system that runs on both small and really large machines.

This popularity of UNIX seems to arise not merely from the intrinsic quality of the system but also from two facts: first, from 1975 Bell Laboratories distributed the product at a nominal price to universities and research laboratories working on defence contracts. Since 1980, the door has been open to all universities, within the USA or not, that have satisfied the required criteria - a subtle means of promotion and a clever way of creating a market.

The second fact is linked with the general evolution of the information technology field. In the past, a program was often written for a specific machine. But the writing of software could not keep pace with progress; hence the need to create an operating system that was independent of the machine. This is why CP/M was produced for microcomputers. For more powerful machines, UNIX responds to the same need; it can be 'ported' to different machines, which is an essential feature for the software applications industry.

Features of UNIX

What then does UNIX offer? For the user, we can list four features that are important for ease of use:

(1) the kernel - a vital part of the system that controls the hardware and software resources,

(2) the hierarchical file system,

(3) a large number of utilities, including

(4) the **shell,** which is a command interpreter and macro programming language.

UNIX offers an extremely rich range of utilities (currently more than 200 for version 7) - tools for program development, management, text data manipulation, database management, graphics, games, etc.

Characteristics of **UNIX**

UNIX was first developed on a minicomputer by its own users, who wanted a nicer system that would meet their needs more satisfactorily. It is relatively compact, but well conceived and powerful. It is a flexible, simple and well thought out system.

In summary

- because of the tree structure of its file system, it is easy to create and manage files
- input/output redirection is simplified as far as possible and is made independent of the underlying hardware as far as it can be
- a single command carries out a single function. But, the facility of the **pipe** enables simple modular commands to be linked to carry out a complex task.
- the power of the shell minimises the need to resort to traditional programming languages. Commands can be put together without knowing how to program (or almost!). This is the art of developing UNIX-like tools with UNIX and for UNIX.

Part 1   A diagonal view of UNIX

1   Starting off

1.0 Session aim

You are going to learn how to begin and end a dialogue with a computer under UNIX: login, password, work session.

First of all, we shall show you how to recover from the errors often made by users at the beginning of their training: how to erase a character or a line, abort an initiated command, etc.

You will be trying a few of the first commands, just to get some hands-on experience of UNIX: **date, who am I, who,** etc.

1.1 Logging on: login

On a single user personal computer, there is no logging on (login or logon). This is not necessary as you are the sole user of the computer system. In a large computer system (mini, super-mini, mega - micro, even) with several simultaneous users, for various control reasons it needs to be established who is working, at what terminal and when.

When your computer is put installed by the person responsible for the computer system (the super-user, in UNIX terminology), the terminal linked to it, if correctly configured, will display on its screen 'login'. Note that one login may hide behind another. While holding down the control key CTRL, press key D (from now on we shall write CTRL-D). You will then obtain 'login' once again.

```
login :                          = CTRL-D pressed
login :                          = system's reply
```

Now, the machine is live, since you had a response from the system. You can now key in your brand new login name that your computer services have given you. Do not forget to press the Return key after the last letter of this name. If you have mistyped, you may get an error message. The system will then ask you to give the correct name. Here is a correct example

```
login : moira                    = your name followed by return
password :                       = system message
```

If you give an incorrect login name, which your UNIX system verifies from a list of users allowed access to the system, you may get a response similar to the following

```
login : mira
Login incorrect                          = system message
login :                                  = start again
```

It may be that your UNIX does not make such a comparison. In which case, there will be no error message and the display will be similar to the first example given above. It will move on to the next line as though the name was accepted.

On the other hand, if no message appears on the next line, you have certainly forgotten to press the Return key (sometimes called Carriage Return or CR). With no Return, the machine does not know whether the line is terminated or not.

If you terminal is connected to a computer by a telephone line via a modem, you must check with your computer services what the link protocol is in order for you to obtain 'login' on your screen. We shall not go into the details of this, since it very much depends on the type of modem and the terminal being used.

1.2 Password: passwd

As you can see from the first example, once you have correctly passed the login line, the system displays another line: password. You now have to key in your password, followed by Return. Do not be surprised if nothing appears on the screen, since a password is usually secret. Everything that you type on your keyboard is first sent to UNIX which then 'echoes' those characters on the screen. UNIX is an active participant, linking your keyboard to the screen. Thus the echo on the screen of what you key in is not, in fact, local. This echoing, then, is not carried out while you type your password.

If you have no password, UNIX will not ask you for one. Note though that you can create one yourself and change it at any time. All you need to use is the command **passwd** which we shall discuss later.

If you make a mistake in keying the password, you will be returned to the login line as shown below. You must then start again.

```
login : moira
password :                               = an error is made
Login incorrect                          = system response
login :                                  = start again
```

If all goes well, you will obtain a set of system messages: the name of your organisation, the news of the day, date, elctronic mail facility, etc. It all depends on the day's events and the super-user's choice. The display may look like this

```
login : moira
password :

4.2 BSD UNIX #34: Thu Jun 20 20:49:03 BST 1985

Welcome to Lancaster Computing VAX-11/750

Sun Jul 20 12:06:33 BST 1986
You have mail
$
```

Note in the preceding example how only the last two lines, which are not internal messages of the organisation, come from UNIX: the date, and your electronic mail.

1.3 Main call symbol: $ prompt
At the beginning of the last line, the $ symbol appears, with an urgently flashing cursor beside it. This character is called the prompt - the call symbol, either waiting or requesting, which means that the UNIX command interpreter, the shell, is ready to work for you. When people speak of being in control, or being handed back control, they are referring to the presence or absence of this symbol. Usually, for the the Bell Laboratories version 7, this is the $ symbol and for UCB versions it is the %. You might have some-thing else, as any symbol can be defined for it. You might want to do it to personalise your dialogue with the machine. In chapter 4 we shall see how to change the main prompt symbol and the secondary prompt which you will meet further on.

1.4 Work session
Once the shell has been invoked, the real work session begins and all kinds of UNIX commands can be accepted. This session lasts until you indicate the end of the work session by sending CTRL-D (no need for Return) to the shell. This is what you have to do to leave the terminal. This signal, which is called end of file, is usually used to signal the end of data coming from the keyboard. If it is used at the shell level, it means that there are no more commands to be handled. The shell will interpret this as the end of the session and will send a fresh 'login' message for a new session. There is therefore no specific command for disconnection, like logout or

logoff, although some UNIX systems do require such a phrase. Even if
the terminal power supply is cut, the virtual session will continue
until the next CTRL-D command is sent. Note that all sequences
signalled by the CTRL key do not appear on the screen as they cannot
be displayed.

```
$                                      = CTRL-D to terminate
login :                                = next, please
```

   It is also possible to disconnect in the following way

```
$ login                                = key these five letters
login :                                = system reply
```

On receiving the keyword **login**, the shell cuts your work session
and sends a message for the start of another session (for you or for
someone else).

   If your terminal uses the telephone, any interruption, voluntary
or otherwise, brings the session to an end.

1.5 Notes on login

Before going further we shall include some remarks on opening a
session (or logging on). UNIX prefers, so far as possible, to work
in lower case letters. This is more restful for the eyes. This
convention applies to the command names and to system messages in
general. But you can use upper case elsewhere, for example in the
names of files and in textual data.

   If you are insistent upon using upper case, the system will
oblige. You simply have to login in upper case. Then, even if you
subsequently enter data in lower case, the echo and response to the
commands will be in upper case. In such cases, it is not possible to
distinguish between two strings of characters that are
orthographically identical but different in letter size. This may
create difficulties. In order to revert to lower case, end the
session with CTRL-D (not with **login**) and begin again.

```
LOGIN : LARGE
PASSWORD :                             = upper case, as you wanted
```

   It is possible that having correctly passed through the login and
password stages, you may get a rather unsympathetic response, followed by login.

```
$ login : quick                        = key name fast
password :                             = ditto password
```

```
No directory                          = system not ready for you
login :
```

This is probably because you got to the terminal before your super-user has had time to prepare the file system for you. Ask him politely how far he has got with this.

1.6 The shell command interpreter

Once you have got the **$** symbol, you can immediately start work by keying whatever command you want. Remember that the commands are, generally speaking, utility programs provided with the UNIX system or programs developed by someone else (soon by you), but recognised by the shell. The shell is the interface between you and the commands.

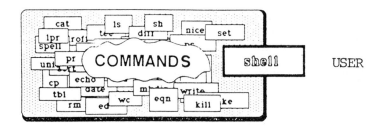

The code program corresponding to a command is held in what is called a file (we shall examine this in detail later). You access a file via the shell, by means of the name assigned to it; in the case of a command, it is found in a file that bears its name. As soon as you key in a sequence of letters, then the Return key, the shell searches for the file corresponding to this name on the disk (files are normally held on disk) or elsewhere. If it finds it, and that file is a command, it executes the instructions found in the file.

We shall try the command that causes the date and time to be displayed, just as we saw at the login stage.

```
$ date                                = key this plus Return
Sun Jul 20 11:31:51 BST 1986          = system reply
$                                     = other command?
```

UNIX foresees everything! Even if we are so tired and confused that we forget our own login name, the following command can help us

```
$ who am I                            = or, 'who are you'
moira      tty02    Jul 20 09:50       = reply from system
$
```

The system replies that 'moira' is working at the terminal called 'tty02'. The use of tty, for teletype, in various operating systems goes back to the days when such devices were used as terminals. This command is useful when you want to know your own identity, if you are working at several terminals at the same time with different names.

It is true that the command does not reflect how it would be written in formal English, but that is how it is. If written correctly, it will not function.

```
$ Who am I?                         = what a purist!
Who: not found                      = not understood
$
```

In order to prove to yourself that you are not the only person slaving away at a terminal, the command **who** will display the names of all the users working at their respective terminals, together with their login time.

```
$ who                               = who is there?
stephen  tty17   Jul 19 20:53
jam      ttyhl   Jul 20 08:15
moira    tty02   Jul 20 09:50       = reply from system
$
```

If you key in a sequence of characters that cannot be a command name, the shell sends an error message. Try making a deliberate error by striking at random the top row of the alphabet keys.

```
$ qwerty                            = 6 letters plus Return
qwerty: not found                   = error is understood
$
```

Even if your keyboard is an 'azerty' type, the problem is the same. The shell is unable to find a file with this name. If you do not get an error message, the name you have typed must exist as a command added locally to your UNIX system. The error message sent by the shell can vary from one command to another. Don't let this error message confuse you, so long as you are subsequently able to obtain the ready symbol **$**. This means that you are again in contact with the shell.

1.7 Correcting a character
As we have just seen, a keying error is of no importance when an isolated command is involved. But it is preferable to correct a

spelling error as soon as it has occurred, or at least before pressing Return. The best way to correct mistakes is to use the **stty**
command (Set TeleTYpe). Try it and pay attention to the line that
contains the word erase in the system's response.

```
$ stty all                          = 7 letters  (and  a  space)
and CR
new tty, speed 9600 baud; -tabs           = reply begins
crt                                       = pay attention
erase   kill    werase rprnt  flush   lnext  ...
#        @       ΔW     ΔR     ΔO      ΔV     ...
$
```

    In this example, the hash **#** must be used as the corrector symbol.
In another system, the second line of the response might differ

```
erase       kill
ΔH          ΔU
```

    Under this system, you have two choices: either press key H while
holding down CTRL (in the message this is shown as ΔH), or use the
left arrow key or the BS (backspace) key, if there is one. You need
to press the key once for each character that has to be removed. On
an old terminal, both the error and its correction remain displayed.

```
$ stty####                          = 4 letters deleted
```

1.8 Correcting a line

What we have just done comes down to erasing a line. The best way of
erasing the current line (that is, the line that you are editing,
before pressing Return) is to use the symbol linked with kill included in the reply to the **stty** command. This is the **@** symbol shown in
the first example of the previous section. Generally, when you use
the erase key in the current line, the cursor positions itself
physically at the next line, but theoretically it is just beside the
$ symbol; in other words, you are always on the current line. Of
course, if you then press the Return key you send a live command to
the shell, and it replies with another **$**.

```
$ Shell will ignore this line @       = a line disappears
```

    <-the cursor flashes here, but you are beside the $, just above

    It should be noted that users may, if they wish, redefine the
character and line erasing symbols, using the same **stty** command.

1.9 Interrupting a command line: DEL

The method described above is useful for correcting keying errors, so long as you deal with them before they are sent to the shell when you press Return. If you do not, you have to cancel what you sent to the shell, especially if the task you have set will require long processing. Depending on the terminal, you need to press a partic- ular key, such as Delete (DEL), Rubout (RUB), Break or CTRL-C. Should your terminal have more than two of these keys, you should check with the supervisor which is the appropriate key to use.

1.10 Several commands on the same line: ;

You are not obliged to use a fresh line for each command. If you have several to key in, you only need to separate them with a semi-colon. It is optional whether you insert a space before and after the semi-colon. The shell will hand you back control after the last command in the line has been executed.

```
$ date; who am I; stty all
Sat Jul 20 11:92:51 BST 1986
moira    tty02  Jul 20 09:50
new tty, speed 9600 baud; -tabs
crt
erase  kill   werase rprnt  flush  lnext  ...
#      @      ∆W     ∆R     ∆O     ∆V     ...
$
```

1.11 Summary

In this first session you have learnt the basic elements you need to converse with UNIX.

You know what you have to do after these lines:

login :   (login name)
password :   (pass word)

You have also learnt the meaning of the following symbols:

$	main call symbol sent by the system
#	character correction
@	current line correction
;	command separator
CTRL-D	end of file; end of session (logout)
CTRL-C, DEL	interrupt commands.

We have tried out these commands:

login	opening and closing a work session
date	date display
who	listing of users currently at work
am I	gives the user's identity.

2 Input and output

2.0 Session aim

You will learn how to create a file by sending the reply of a command that you typed to it; this is standard output redirection.

We shall also introduce a limited number of commands relating to created files. These are display of contents, listing of names, duplication or destruction of these files, etc.

Finally, we shall examine some of the symbols that are specific to UNIX, that is, some of the special characters (also called meta-characters) that will often be of help in your work.

2.1 Standard input and output

Up until now, we have not been concerned with the medium of output, and the replies to commands were displayed on the screen. More precisely, the commands did not send the results to the screen, they sent them to a place called standard output. It is up to the shell to connect the standard output to an output medium, to a file or to another command, according to the user's requirements. If the output is not specified, the shell takes the screen to be the standard output.

Similarly, the system automatically recognises the keyboard as the input medium, even if it is not stated explicitly. Again it is the shell that establishes the link between the standard input, either with the keyboard, with a file or again with another command

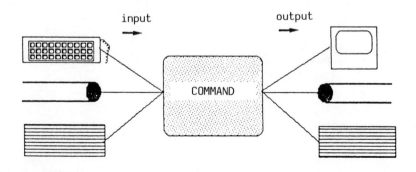

using a pipe (see section 9.1). The user therefore has the choice, when calling the command, of whether to specify the input of his choice or leave it to the default medium.

There is also the error output. When the system detects an incorrect command, an error message is normally sent to the screen, but it can also be sent to a file if necessary.

How is it possible to interchange standard inputs and/or outputs so easily? The key to this question lies in the fact that all the media for inputting or outputting data have the status of files. The characteristics of each input/output device are described in a special file. Hence, using these peripherals amounts to the same as accessing the special files that are assigned to them. It is simply a question of swapping between files (standard, special or ordinary).

2.2 Redirecting output to a file: >

In order to study this problem, we shall take the **echo** command which acts like a parrot. This command repeats on the standard output, for example the screen, the string of characters placed after it. For input data, it is preferable to place these characters or words within quotes.

```
$ echo "echo echo echo"        = what an interesting acoustic effect
echo echo echo                 = quite so
$
```

We can send these echoes to a file, if we use the redirection symbol > followed by the name of the file in which we want to store the repeated string. Note that the > symbol has no mathematical or logical significance; it simply means that everything on the left of the symbol goes to the right. Just imagine it to be an arrow point-ing to the right. A space before and after > is optional.

```
$ echo "one two three" > vals        = sends all to 'vals'
$
```

We have therefore redirected the output of the command to a file. A tiny file called **vals** has been created.

The length of a file name is restricted to 14 characters. Although inadvisable, it is not forbidden to use the special meta-character symbols (cf 2.10) as part of a file name; if you do, you may subsequently have difficulty when you try to manipulate such files.

Any command written to the standard output can be redirected. In the following examples, the output command **who am** I goes to the file called **amnesia** and the reply to the **who** command goes to the file called **kitty**.

```
$ who am I > amnesia
$ who > kitty
$
```

2.3 Display the contents of a file: cat

When you create a file by command output redirection, it is usual to want to verify the contents. The **cat** command takes care of this. The name is extracted from the word concatenation. **cat** reads the files in sequence, concatenates them and displays the result on the standard output. Obviously, any request to display a nonexistent file will produce an error message.

```
$ cat vals                              = let's look at this file
one two three
$ cat sesame                            = open Sesame
sesame: No such file or directory       = UNIX is not a magician
$
```

There is nothing to prevent you from displaying several existing files or placing them in a single file, by keying the following commands

```
$ cat file1 file2 ...                   = (for display)
$ cat file1 file2 ... > grofile         = (to regroup)
```

2.4 Adding information at the end of a file: >>

It is often necessary to add new data to that already held in a file. But first let us look at the following examples

```
$ echo "This is very useful" > useful   = note the quotes
$ cat useful
This is very useful
$ echo "and so is this" > useful; cat useful
and so is this
$
```

Here the first contents of the file have been accidentally overwritten by the second **echo** redirected to the same file. In order to retain the first line of the file we should have used the add symbol >> instead of >.

```
$ echo "This is very useful" > useful
$ echo "and so is this" >> useful        = add
$ cat useful
This very useful
and so is this
$
```

You have used **echo** twice to record this information. The same effect can be obtained using only one **echo.**

```
$ echo "test for writing            = first line
> two lines at once"                = second line
test for writing                    = output
two lines at once
$
```

The > symbol at the beginning of the line, shown above, is the secondary prompt of the shell. The shell waits for the rest of the line of commands which was not terminated. There is no possibility of confusion between the secondary prompt and the redirection command, because the prompt is sent by the shell, whereas the redirection is specified by the user.

2.5 Redirecting standard input: <
To understand standard input redirection, we shall take the **rev** command which inverts the line: head to tail and tail to head. It reads the data at the standard input and sends the results to the standard output.

```
$ rev                                = command name and CR
abcdefgh                             = key in
hgfedcba                             = this is the result
$                                    = CTRL-D to exit
```

As with **echo** above, let us write a sentence to a file

```
$ echo "madam I'm adam" > anywhere
```

We can now invert the contents of that file by redirecting the file to the **rev** command.

```
$ rev < anywhere
mada m'I madam                       = the reply
$
```

2.6 Listing file names: ls

To verify the list of our files, we use the **ls** command which displays the names of existing files. As shown below, the names are sorted into increasing alphabetical order. We shall see later that this command offers options that allow different information about the files to be obtained.

```
$ ls                                = let's list our customers
amnesia
anywhere
kitty
useful
vals
$                                   = that's all for now
```

2.7 Copying a file

2.7.1 With cp

The **cp** command sees to the task of CoPying. The first argument is the name of the file to be copied and the second is the name of the file that is to contain the copy.

```
$ cp vals musette                   = vals to musette
$ cat musette
one two three
$
```

2.7.2 With cat

The **cat** command can carry out a similar task. To do this, you simply have to mention the name of a file that exists and redirect its contents to another file, instead of leaving it displayed on the screen, which is the implicit output.

```
$ cat vals                          = display vals
one two three
$
```

and another **cat** for the copy in a new file that will be created as soon as the shell analyses the > symbol.

```
$ cat vals > viennese               = vals is copied to viennese
$ cat viennese                      = verify
one two three
$
```

We now merge the two files.

```
$ cat vals >> viennese              = vals + viennese = ?
$ cat viennese                      = let's see the result
one two three
one two three
$                                   = contents added
```

What distinguishes the **cp** from the **cat** command is first the fact that **cp** does not use standard output; the file names have to be named explicitly, both original and copy. Second, **cp** copies both the contents and the status of the file (cf 8.2), whereas **cat** only reproduces the contents.

Remember too that for both commands an output file will be created, if there is not one already. If there is, the previous contents will be overwritten by the new.

2.8 Changing a file name: mv
You can change the name of a file with the **mv** (MoVe) command. In contrast to copying with **cat** or **cp, mv** leaves no copy behind it.

```
$ mv vals 123
$
```

The **vals** file has taken the name 123 as we see when we list with **ls**

```
$ ls
123
amnesia
anywhere
kitty
musette
useful
viennese
$
```

Although not disallowed, it is inadvisable to name a file with numerals alone, so we will revert to the original name.

```
$ mv 123 vals
$
```

2.9 Destroying a file: rm
If we multiply copies, sooner or later we shall need to do some

housekeeping by getting rid of useless files. **rm** (ReMove) is the
command used.   We shall now remove some of our existing files.

```
$ rm vals viennese                    = two files are removed
$ ls                                  = list remaining files
amnesia
anywhere
kitty
musette
useful
$
```

   Of course, if we try to remove a file that does not exist, we
shall get an error message.

```
$ rm ovni
rm: ovni nonexistent                  = naturally
$
```

   Now try this

```
$ rm a*
$
```

and verify what has happened with **ls**

```
$ ls
kitty
musette
useful
$
```

   You have lost two files. Why?

2.10 Generic metacharacters

Characters that have a special meaning are called metacharacters. In
the above example, the * symbol is used to represent part of the
name of a file, in the case of "mnesia" and "nywhere". The shell
generates the abbreviated part by examining all the file names
recorded in your current workspace (current directory, see following
session).
   We have seen that the asterisk can be used in place of a string
of variable length, but take care that this length can be zero. For
example, "*a" can designate "ta", "beta", but also "a" by itself.

Similarly, the string "a*" can represent "alpha" as well as "a". The expression "*a*b*" can correspond to "samba", but also to "ab".

This * symbol can also designate all the files in the current workspace. Here is an example not to be followed, for if you do you will lose all the files on which you have spent so much time. Fortunately, in this case this would not be serious.

```
$ rm *                          = think about it!
```

For those who wish to try **rm ***, but not too painfully, we suggest using the **-i** (interactive) option, which lists all the files, one by one in alphabetical order. You reply with **y** or **n** depending on your choice. This option is useful for destroying files whose name contains invisible or unprintable characters owing to a keying error.

```
$ rm -i *                       = reply as you wish
kitty:
```

In contrast, the question mark **?** is less disastrous; it represents any character in the file name. To illustrate this, we shall create two files **musette1** and **musette2**.

```
$ mv musette musette1           = change name
$ cp musette1 musette2          = duplicate
$ ls                            = here are the files
kitty
musette1
musette2
useful
$
```

Now see the effect of **?** in the **rm** command.

```
$ rm musette?
$ ls
kitty
useful
$
```

So, we have removed two files at a stroke. What is more, a single **?** can designate single letter files, if they exist. The next command line only relates to two-character file names, which do not exist here.

```
$ rm ??
rm: ?? nonexistent                        = system message
$
```

Note in this reply that since the ?? does not refer to any file, the shell has interpreted these symbols as a literal string. This is a general rule in the expansion of generic metacharacters.

These metacharacters are not reserved for **rm**; they can be used anywhere to designate files.

2.11 Summary
In this session we have examined the elements listed below. Go back over them if you are not quite familiar with them.

Concepts on standard peripherals and their redirection. Remember the following symbols:

```
>       send a command output to a file
>>      add a command output to a file
<       take data from a file
```

We have studied the following common commands:

echo   obtain the echo of data
cat   display, concatenate, copy files
cp   copy a file
ls   list file names
mv   change a file name
rm   destroy a file
          interactive option **−i**

The system uses the secondary prompt > if the command line is incomplete.

The following generic metacharacters enable file names to be generated:

```
*     represents any string of characters (including an empty string)
?     represents a single character.
```

3 Files and directories

3.0 Session aim
We shall now study the UNIX file system, which has a tree structure. We shall consider the following concepts: home directory, current directory, root directory.

At the same time, we shall look at the commands that are necessary to change current directory **cd**, recognise the complete path of the current directory from the root **pwd**, and create a directory **mkdir**.

Finally, we will learn the special symbols that refer to directories.

3.1 What is a directory?
Under UNIX, the file system is organised in a tree structure. As an example, think of your own family tree.

In the UNIX tree of files and directories there is a root, branches and leaves. A leaf corresponds to a file. A node, from which both leaves and branches grow, is called a directory. A directory is therefore a place where we can create files and sub-directories.

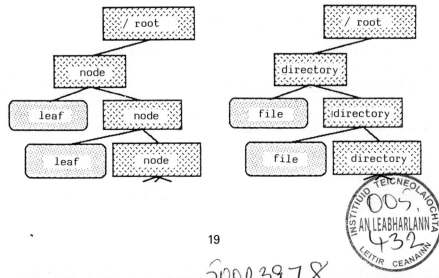

3.2 Home directory

When you have obtained your authorisation to access the UNIX system, the super-user has created what is called a home directory that bears your login name. As soon as you open the work session, the shell puts you automatically in your home directory, from which small branches (sub-directories) and leaves (files) can be developed.

3.3 Work directory

In the previous session, in this home directory we have created files, displayed them, then listed their names, calling the appropriate commands. In short, we have worked in the home directory.

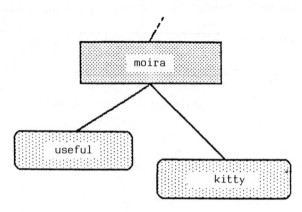

Here, Moira has used her home directory as the current directory, sometimes known as the working directory. Whereas the home directory is defined, the current directory is not. We can go from one directory to another, as required, as we shall see later.

3.4 Recognising the current directory: pwd

For the time being, this is not really necessary for us to know, but after many changes of current directory, one can easily lose track of where one is. The **pwd** (print pathname of working directory) command provides us with the complete path of the current directory beginning at the root of the file system. In the reply to the command we shall find on the extreme right the name of the current directory, the root at the beginning, and in between all the intermediate directories in hierarchical order.

```
$ pwd                          = where are we?
/users/moira                   = so that's where we were
$
```

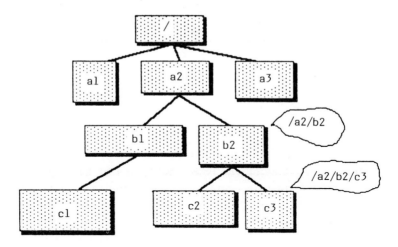

No doubt the reply to this command will be displayed differently on your terminal, especially the directory names which vary from one system to another. But the essentials are always happily similar.

The first oblique bar (slash) shows the root of the file system in UNIX. This is the departure point for all the directories and files. The first directory after the root is **users** in this example. The second slash is a delimiter which separates the **users** directory from the **moira** directory, which is the current directory.

3.5 Changing current directory (1): cd

In order to shift from one directory to another, we shall use the **cd** (change working directory) command. It will allow us to return to the home directory from any directory. Since we have not yet moved from the home directory, its effect is not very spectacular at this point. We shall benefit from it later.

```
$ cd                            = let's go home
$ pwd                           = we were not lost
/users/moira                    = here we are
$
```

To place ourselves in a directory, we have to indicate immed- iately after the **cd** the complete path from the root to the directory that we want to reach.

```
$ cd /users                     = we want to go to the next stage up
$ pwd                           = where are we?
/users                          = we are there
$
```

We can display what there is in the **users** directory just above the home directory by using **ls**.

```
$ ls /users
fred
jam
moira
yuki
$
```

This is the list of the home directories of our system's users. What is yours? In this example, we have provided the **ls** command with the complete directory pathway, which is not essential, since we are at the **users** level. However, in this way we can obtain the listing of any directory, without changing the current directory. This applies for all commands, for example, **cat, cp, mv, rm**, etc.

Let us climb higher to see what we find.

```
$ cd /                          = let's go to the top
$ pwd                           = where are we?
/                               = this is the end of the line
$
```

We will try **ls** again to look at the directories belonging to the root, just to satisfy our curiosity.

```
$ ls                            = same as 'ls /'
bin
boot
dev
etc
lib
mnt
tmp
users
usr
$
```

On your UNIX the reply may differ, but you should find these included in your list. These directories hold all the important UNIX files. For example, in the **bin** directory you will find the frequently used commands, such as **cat, cp, ls,** etc.

```
$ ls /bin
adb
as
awk
cat
cc
chgrp
chmod
cmp
cp
```

Now that we are familiar with the file system directories, we can describe the tree that represents the relationship between the directories and files that have appeared in our examples.

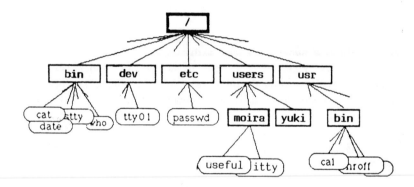

3.6 Directory metacharacters (special characters)

There is an abbreviation to indicate a directory immediately above the current directory. A double period .. is used. When used in conjunction with the **cd** command this convention is of practical value for going up through the directories. There must be a space between **cd** and ...

```
$ cd ; pwd
/users/moira
$ cd..                          = we start
cd..: not found                 = good start!
$
```

Don't be put off. Put a space between **cd** and .. and try again.

```
$ cd .. ; pwd                         = again
/users                                = yes
$ cd ; pwd                            = back home
/users/moira
$ cd ../.. ; pwd                      = climb 2 levels
/                                     = the top
$
```

In the last command line, the first two periods indicate the directory above the one to the right of the slash, which is itself above the current directory. A space before or after the slash would cause an error.

There is another symbol that relates to the directory. This is the single period . which represents the current directory. It is often used with commands to recopy files between the current directory and another directory (cf 3.9).

3.7 Creating a sub-directory: mkdir

We have now reached the point where we can create our own directories. The command for this operation is **mkdir** (MaKe a DIRectory). The command must have an argument, that is, a directory name that we want to create.

```
$ cd ; pwd ; ls                       = verify everything
/users/moira                          = home
kitty
useful
$
```

That was just revision.

```
$ mkdir puss.1                        = first offspring
$ mkdir puss.2                        = second offspring
$ ls
kitty
puss.1                                = entry recorded
puss.2
useful
$
```

For the moment, these two sub-directories are empty. We will now send to **puss.1** a file containing some information, for example, its date of birth.

```
$ date > kitty                        = recycle file
$ mv kitty birthday                   = change name
$
$ cp birthday puss.1                  = note period
$ ls puss.1
birthday                              = puss.1 contains a file
$
```

In the second command line, the file **birthday**, previously **kitty** in the current directory **moira**, has been duplicated in the sub-directory **puss.1**, keeping the same file name. To verify that the command has executed correctly, we have listed all the file names in the directory. At present, there is only one.

   Of course, this could have been achieved by this simple command line.

```
$ date > puss.1/birthday
$
```

3.8 More on changing directory (2): cd
We will go down from the **moira** home directory to the target sub-directory **puss.1**.

```
$ cd ; pwd
/users/moira                          = home
$ cd puss.1 ; pwd                     = we descend
/users/moira/puss.1
$
```

   The movement is always vertical.

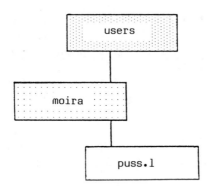

   On the other hand, we cannot go directly from the **puss.1**
directory to **puss.2**, because they are two different branches from
the same parent directory.

```
$ pwd
/users/moira/puss.1
$ cd puss.2
puss.2: bad directory              = error
$
```

We need to go back to the parent directory and from there indicate
the path to be taken to the target directory. The **cd** command does
not recognise horizontal movement.

```
$ cd ../puss.2                     = up and down
$ pwd
/users/moira/puss.2                = here we are
$
```

In our case, this is not so complicated. We just have to go up from
the current directory to the higher **moira** level using the double
period, then indicate the rest of the path, which is simply **puss.2**.

   So far it has been customary to indicate the complete pathway of
the directory to the **cd** command; we specified this path from the
root beginning with a slash. In this last example we used another
method of giving the directory coordinates, by indicating the
relative target address, with reference to the current directory;
the path does not begin with a slash. To summarise
- absolute address : path from the root
- relative address : path from the current directory.

3.9 Copying a file from one directory to another: cp
Using the **cp** command, we can copy the **birthday** file of the higher
directory into this directory (**puss.2**). Pay close attention to the
metacharacters, the period and two periods.

```
$ pwd
/users/moira/puss.2
$ cp ../birthday .                 = note single period
$ ls
birthday
$
```

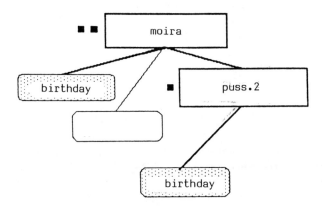

The second operation is to copy the file **useful** into this same
directory, but changing its name, into say, **memory.**

```
$ cp ../useful ./memory                    = note periods
$ ls
birthday
memory
$
```

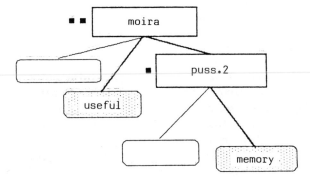

You can carry out the same operations, with the complete address.
The command line **cp** can be

```
$ cp /users/moira/birthday /users/moira/puss.2
$ cp /users/moira/useful /users/moira/puss.2/memory
$
```

Long strings of characters like these are not only taxing to type
but also subject to error. The shell offers variables to solve this
problem; you can change the complicated element into a variable and
then refer to the contents by using the variable. In the examples

below, the variable is to the left of the equals sign and the
contents are to the right.

```
$ depart=/users/moira
$ arrive=/users/moira/puss.2
$
```

   To use these variables in a line of commands, you place a **$** in
front of them. When it analyses the command line, the shell replaces
the variable with its contents. Once defined, the variable can be
used throughout the work session.

```
$ echo $arrive                    = what does this variable contain?
/users/moira/puss.2               = this
$
```

   With these variables, the first command line executing the copy
then becomes

```
$ cp $depart/birthday $arrive
$
```

To recapitulate
- cp original file copied file
- cp file(s) directory

3.10 Transferring a file from one directory to another: mv
You can use **mv**, which we have already met in session 2, to transfer
one or more files from one directory to another. The syntax is
exactly the same as that of **cp**. This command first copies the specified file(s), then destroys the original. But, until we have
mastered this, it is better to use **cp** followed by **rm**.

3.11 Changing a directory name: mv
This same command also allows you to change the name of a directory
that is yours, just like a file.

```
$ mv /users/moira/puss.1 /users/moira/fatcat        = quite a change
$
```

3.12 Destroy a file: rmdir
When reorganising directories, it is sometimes necessary to destroy
a directory whose contents (files) have been copied elsewhere. For

this we have to
- destroy all the files in it
- put ourselves in the parent directory.

```
$ pwd
/users/moira/fatcat
$ rm *                                        = that's alarming
$ rmdir fatcat                                = run!
rmdir: fatcat: No such file or directory      = position error
$ cd ..                                        = again
$ rmdir fatcat
$                                              = goodbye
```

3.13 Identifying directories and files: ls -l
In the examples above, we were distinguishing implicitly between
files and directories by relying on our memory, which becomes weaker
with the passing seconds. The **ls** command, with the **-l** (long) option,
displays all the information on the files and sub-directories,
including the differences between files and directories; this is all
we are interested in at the moment. Note that the UNIX command
options are very often (but not always) preceded by a dash, without
a space between it and the option.

```
$ cd ; pwd                                    = return home
/users/moira
$ ls -l
total 3
-r--r--r-- 1 moira        459 Jul 20 14:11 anywhere
-rw-r--r-- 1 moira         29 Jul 20 14:15 birthday
drwxr-xr-x 2 moira        512 Jul 20 14:18 puss.2
$
```

Let us concentrate only on the beginning of each line of the
reply. The last line begins with letter **d** (directory). This is
therefore how we identify directories whose name is found at the end
of the line; when there is a dash instead of this letter this means
that we are only talking about an ordinary file. As for the rest of
the information, we shall return to this in session 8.

3.14 Summary
In this session we have learnt the preliminary concepts of the system of files and directories, namely

- directory
- home directory

- current or working directory
- the tree structure of the file system
- the complete pathway of a directory and a file

New commands, or previously introduced ones with new options

pwd   display the complete pathway of the directory
cd   change current directory
ls -l list file names with detailed information
cp   copy files into different directories
mv   transfer one or more files from one directory to another;
           change name of directory
rmdir destroy a directory.

The following shell variables were introduced

a=bb   load bb into variable a
$a   contents of variable a

We have also met the metacharacters that relate to directories

.   current directory
..   immediate parent directory.

4 Text editor

4.0 Session aim
First we shall examine the basic concepts of the text editor; then the sub-commands of the editor, **ex.**
These will show you how to write, display, alter or remove a section of text in a file.

4.1 Text editing
We now know how to prepare a small file containing a few words using the **echo** command. Nothing stands in the way of its being used to add dozens of lines. The same can be achieved with the **cat** command.

For a change, let's use an extract of some poetry. The text that we key in will go into the file called Wordsworth.

```
$ cat > Wordsworth            = what we key will go to 'Wordsworth'
Eearth has not anything to show more fair:
Dull would he be of soul who could pass by
<- CTRL-D pressed here        = CTRL-D to exit
$
```

The novelty in using **cat** here lies in the absence of a file to be displayed; **cat** then reads its standard input, the keyboard.

As you will have noticed, there is a keying error in the first line. If we were not to correct that error with the **@** or **#** before pressing Return, we would have to start again by going back to the first line of the example, and type all the text again.

4.2 Text editors
The procedure required in the previous section is annoying when lengthy text is involved. The text editor solves this problem by allowing you to add or remove lines, alter part of a string, etc. Depending on the version you have, UNIX offers several text editors: **ed, ex, vi, sed.**

The current editors, for example **vi** in the versions derived from UCB UNIX, allow the cursor to be moved in all four directions by means of special keys. The screen is considered to be a kind of page

31

on   which   you write your text. This screen oriented editor requires
terminals capable of supporting cursor movement.

   Line editors are oriented towards the editing of lines and all
action is carried out on the basis of lines. This means that a line
can always be located through a pointer which contains the current
line number. However, it is less easy to find a character within a
line, because there is no character pointer to position itself on a
particular letter. This type of line editor is now obsolete.

   However, it is worth examining **ex** for two reasons. Firstly, if
you only have access to a terminal unable to support two-dimensional
cursor movement. Secondly, UNIX supports a family of editors. **ex**
(and **edit**, a simpler variant of **ex**) and **ed** are line editors of
similar function; they share many commands. **ex** forms the basis of **vi**
(see session 25); therefore, all the line oriented commands that we
learn in our study of **ex** will serve us equally well in our use of
vi.

4.3 Editing and writing modes
In an interactive editor, there are two different methods of
operation: editing mode and writing mode. In editing mode, text that
has already been input can be manipulated using various commands
designated by a single character. In contrast, in writing mode,
everything that you key in is taken to be data input and no command
is recognised. The correction symbols operate in both modes.

4.4 Temporary file for editor
As we have already seen, the data on which the editor must operate
is held in a file located on disk. Each time that you call the
editor, **ex** creates a temporary working file in the directory **/tmp**,
which serves to receive new data or the contents of an existing
file.

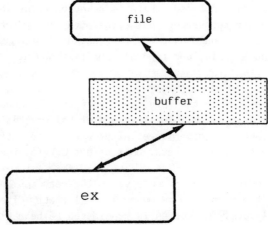

4.5 Text editor ex

ex is one of the standard text editors of UNIX. We shall now give a brief overview of it, giving the minimum commands required to write a piece of text and make any necessary corrections to it.

When you key **ex**, you enter the editing mode. As mentioned above, you now have various sub-commands available to you. These commands are single characters.

```
$ ex                              = call ex
:                                 = note ':' prompt for ex
```

In some versions, some symbol, perhaps an asterisk, will appear as the prompt at the beginning of the line, when in edit mode.

4.5.1 Edit a file: e

We will edit our **Wordsworth** file. To call it, you key the letter **e** followed by a space and then the file name.

```
:e Wordsworth
"Wordsworth" 2 lines, 86 characters
                              = number of lines and characters  read
```

We have asked the editor to read the **Wordsworth** file held on the disk. The command replied that it has copied the two lines, consisting of 86 characters, that it found in that file into the workspace. The number of characters includes the visible letters as well as the invisible spaces and carriage returns. It depends on how you keyed in the text in the first place.

If the editor queries the existence of the file, it is telling you that the file you have named must be a new file, because it has not been able to find one with this name. If there is a mistake in the name, you need to start again with the correct name.

```
:e wordsworth
"wordsworth" No such file or directory        = new file?
:e Wordsworth
"Wordsworth" 2 lines, 86 characters
                              = number of lines and characters read
```

4.5.2 Pointing to one or more lines

When the contents of a file are copied into the workspace, the line pointer is found at the end of the text. In order to move this pointer somewhere else, you simply key in the number of the line

that you want and press Return. This will display the line. To go to
the next line, you simply press Return. And so on; you can step
through the text line by line to the end.

Quite often you may want to find several lines in succession. To
do this, you specify the two boundary numbers, separated by a comma.
For example, 2,5 means 'from line 2 to 5' and 1,$ 'from line 1 to
the end'. The $ represents the last line here; within **ex** it does not
have its shell meaning.

4.5.3 Display all or part of the file: p
You can display all the text in the temporary file at once, by
combining the method described in the previous section with the
display function **p** (print).

```
:1,$p                                    = let's look at everything
Eearth has not anything to show more fair:
Dull would he be of soul who could pass by
```

Now, press Return to see the effect. You will get an end-of-file
message. This means that the line pointer had already got to the end
of the work file, after execution of the command line "1,$p". Your
carriage return wanted to send this pointer further, which is
impossible.

4.5.4 Replace one string with another: s/one_string/another/
We now need to find the line in which we have made an error and
correct with the substitution command.

```
:1                                       = equivalent to lp
Eearth has not anything to show more fair:
:s/Eearth/Earth/p                        = correct and display
Earth has not anything to show more fair:
```

The function of the first letter **s** is to replace the first string
of characters delimited by the slashes with another string which
follows, and which also terminates with a slash.

In the **ed,** to find out if the correction has been successful, we
use the **p** command, since **s** does not display the alteration. Usually,
we use the **s** and **p** functions on the same command line, as above.

If you make an error in the string to be corrected (the first
string), the alteration will not be made. Because **ex** is unable to
identify the substitution place on the line, it abandons the operation, and produces a suitable error message.

```
:s/had/has/
Substitute pattern match failed
```

4.5.5 Entering data: a

If you want to continue text input, you need to use the **a** (add) command at the beginning of the line, followed by Return. This marks your entry to the write mode. Everything now keyed will be accepted as data. Each time your press Return, a line is terminated; even if you begin the line with a Return, for **ex** it is still a line, just like a typewriter.

To exit the write mode, you indicate the end of data with a period . at the beginning of the line, followed by Return. You are now back in the edit mode where commands are recognised. Never forget this period - it can be a trap!

If there is any element, a space for example, in front of or after the period, the line will be taken to be a line of data.

To confirm that you have in fact left the input mode for the the edit mode, press key **p** which will display the last line entered, or press Return which will give you an "at end-of-file" message.

If this does not happen, you are still in write mode. To exit from this, you must carefully insert the period at the beginning of the line, followed by Return and nothing more.

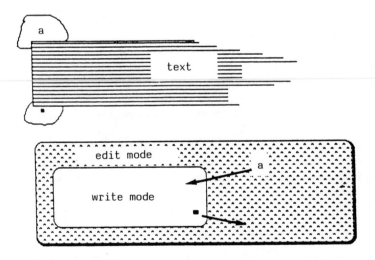

```
:$
Dull would he be of soul who could pass by
:a                                  = the command
A sight so touching in its majecty:
This City now doth, like a garment, wear
```

All bright and glittering in the smokeless air,
The beauty of the morning; silent, bare.

                                  = note the period

4.5.6 Question mark ?

In the **ed** editor, the question mark is a kind of abbreviated error
message; it indicates that you have sent an unrecognisable or impro-
per command. This is no cause for embarrassment, it is a good sign,
because **ed** has replied.

   Never hesitate to press Return if you are in edit mode; it costs
nothing to have yourself presented with a succession of question
marks.

   On the other hand, there is cause for concern if no symbol
appears after repeated pressing of Return. You must be in write mode
and you have inserted lines with each keystroke. This happens if you
forget to come out of write mode.

4.5.7 Destroy a line: d

If we see that a line does not belong in this verse, it is convenient, in order to remove it, to correct it and then destroy it.

:/bright/   = find this line
All bright and glittering in the smokeless air,
:d   = line destroyed
The beauty of the morning; silent, bare.

   If you have obtained an error message, the search has been un-
successful because of incorrect specification of the search string;
this only works when the target string is faithfully reproduced.
:/blight/
Address search hit BOTTOM without matching pattern

   A string enclosed by two slashes, followed by Return, places us
on the line containing this sequence of characters. The d (destroy)
command followed by Return erases the corrected line. Usually, these
two operations are done at once

:/bright/d

   To remove several consecutive lines, the method is similar to the
operation of the **1,$p** command line. The numbers of the first and
last line are given, followed by **d** instead of **p.**

3,$d@

   The command line destroying the third to the last line has been cancelled at the last minute with the command that removes the current line. Before saving this file, let us look at its present contents.

```
:1,$p
```
Earth has not anything to show more fair:
Dull would he be of soul who could pass by
A sight so touching in its majesty:
This City now doth, like a garment, wear
The beauty of the morning; silent, bare.

If an unfortunate incident occurs at the end of input mode (with **a**), you will find some trace of it after the last line of text: either an empty line, a line with a single badly placed period, or command **p** that has not worked. The error must be eliminated. At this stage, our advice is to count back yourself to the incorrect line and then erase everything after it.

4.5.8 Saving a file: **w**
The text is now ready. We need to save the perfect version which is at present held in a temporary working file. The **w** (write) command sees to this. It will replace the original contents (created with **cat**) with the new (obtained under **ex**) and will display the total number of characters in this file.

```
:w                                      = write to the file
"Wordsworth" 5 lines, 203 characters
                         = number of lines and characters written
```

When carrying out a long piece of editing, it is advisable to use **w** from time to time as a protection against any incident, such as a power failure.

4.5.9 Quit ex: **q**
All has gone well, you can now exit the editor to re-enter the shell environment, by using the **q** (quit) command. If this command generates a "No write since last change" message, you must have made other changes after the last save using **w**. If you do not want to save them, press **q** again; otherwise press **w** before pressing **q**.

```
:q                                      = and CR
$                                       = it's done
```

4.6 Summary

We have outlined the basic principles of the text editor ex
- it is a line-oriented text editor
- it uses a temporary working file
- there are two operating modes: write and edit
- commands are functional in edit mode.

   We have learnt, under **ex,** how to alter an existing file or to
create a new file, using the following commands

a   data input
d   destroy one or more lines
e   edit a file
p   display lines
s   replace a character string
w   save a file
q   quit editor
q!   quit editor, ignoring changes made since last write.

   You also know the meaning of

.   exit write mode
1,$ designate first to last line
?   syntax error (within **ed**)

5 Text formatter

5.0 Aim of session

We now enter the word processing field. After a short theoretical discussion on the processing of textual data, we shall review the **nroff** text processor, first with its ordinary instructions, and then with the **ms** macro instructions.

5.1 Word processing

You will already be familiar with the concept of word processing software that allows textual data to be displayed on a screen as it is keyed in. If necessary, the text can be corrected by means of keys with special functions. The screen immediately presents you with the words and sentences just as they will be printed out. There is no apparent separation between the keying in and the representation of the data. This type of program is called a word processor in the current sense of the term.

5.2 Text processors

Under UNIX, the situation is somewhat different. Usually, the data is captured by a text editor, as we have just seen. The task of embellishment is carried out by specialised processors, such as **nroff** and **troff**. You are therefore unable to visualise the effect of the processing in real time. This is why the term 'text formatter' is used in UNIX documentation.

UNIX also contains the mathematical formulae preprocessors **eqn** and **neqn**, as well as the table preprocessor **tbl**. The processors work according to the same concept as those of the text formatters; they must be called, as their names indicate, before formatting the text.

5.3 nroff and troff processors

The difference between these two processors lies principally in the type of print output. **nroff** only requires a printer, whereas **troff** (not discussed in this book) is intended for professional use with typesetting equipment. The best examples of **troff** are the UNIX documentation and the Bell System Technical Journal which, in addition to text, contain drawings and photographs prepared with this processor.

So far as the name **nroff** is concerned, it goes back to the time when similar software was developed by J. Salzer of MIT under the name **roff.** This may well be a contraction of the expression 'run off' (print out), with the addition of n for New.

5.4 nroff: advantages and disadvantages
nroff is certainly not very attractive for producing short letters, but it is better for dealing with lengthy text.

It also has the advantage of not requiring a sophisticated terminal, for input or output.

Lastly, **nroff** is not merely a simple program for text formatting; it allows the user to create his own formatting directives.

5.5 Basic principle of nroff
In order to operate properly, **nroff** needs to be told the name of the file containing the textual data and be provided with all details for processing. You may think that this is rather demanding, but fortunately the normal parameters have a default standard value for items such as margins, number of lines per page, line length, etc. We shall experiment now with a section of text using **nroff.**

```
$ ex
:e Edinburgh                         = file name
"Edinburgh" No such file or directory   = new file
:a                                   = start of text
EDINBURGH

Edinburgh, the capital of Scotland,
is a fine old city
built partly in the valley of the River Leith
and partly on the rolling hills
which surround it.
The city is dominated by the castle,
an ancient fortress standing on the summit
of a massive rock, which has been the scene of
many battles and sieges
throughout centuries of Scottish history.
Today, what remains of the original castle
is preserved as a museum piece and
a home for military relics.
.
:w                                   = end of text; save
"Edinburgh" [New file] 15 lines, 462 characters
```

```
:q                                  = quit ex
$
```

Our material is now ready to be processed by **nroff**, as shown
below.

```
$ nroff Edinburgh                   = command line
EDINBURGH                           = output starts at this line
```

Edinburgh, the capital of Scotland, is a fine old city built partly
in the valley of the River Leith and partly on the rolling hills
which surround it. The city is dominated by the castle, an ancient
fortress standing on the summit of a massive rock, which has been
the scene of many battles and sieges throughout centuries of
Scottish history.   Today, what remains of the original castle is
preserved as a museum piece and a home for military relics.

This is fairly satisfactory, but there are some more improvements
that could be made.

5.6 Ordinary nroff instructions

An instruction line begins with a period . at the beginning of the
line. This tells **nroff** that the following material is a processing
instruction. The instruction line is therefore an independent line
in the text. The instruction, in the form of a two-letter, lower
case abbreviation appears immediately after the period. If this
instruction takes an argument, this is placed after the instruction,
separated by a space. Here are some examples

```
.ce 2    centre two lines of text
.nh      no hyphenation
.ll 40   line length 40 characters
.pl 66   page length 66 lines
.po 10   page offset (left margin) 10 characters
.sp 2    two line space
```

We will now insert some of these instructions into our Edinburgh
file under **ex**. Be careful to distinguish accurately between 0 (the
letter) and 0 (the number zero), and between 1 (small letter l) and
I (capital I) or 1 (number one).

```
$ ex Edinburgh
"Edinburgh" 15 lines, 462 characters        = lines & chars read
:0a                                         = add after line 0
.nh                                         = nroff instruction
.ll 40                                      = nroff instruction
.ce 1                                       = nroff instruction
.                                           = end of text addition
:/EDINBURGH/                                = find this line
EDINBURGH                                   = line displayed
:a                                          = add again
.sp 3                                       = nroff instruction
.                                           = end of addition
:wq                                         = write and quit
"Edinburgh" 19 lines, 485 characters        = lines & chars written
$
```

Note how differently the text is displayed as a result of these instructions. Do not be concerned if there is no immediate result when you send your command. The task set will not be completed in a flash; the delay will depend on the number of other users and what they are doing.

```
$ nroff Edinburgh                       = here is the result
              EDINBURGH
```

Edinburgh, the capital of Scotland, is a
fine old city built partly in the valley
of the River Leith and partly on the
rolling hills which surround it. The
city is dominated by the castle, an
ancient fortress standing on the summit
of a massive rock, which has been the
scene of many battles and sieges
throughout centuries of Scottish
history. Today, what remains of the
original castle is preserved as a museum
piece and a home for military relics.

5.7 ms macro instructions

For standard text formatting use, UNIX offers several **macro** libraries. These are a sort of mini subroutine written in the **nroff** programming language hinted at earlier. There are several well known macros, all beginning with m, such as **me**, **mn**, **ms**, **mv**, etc. We are especially interested in the **ms** standard macros, from the point of view of their general utility.

The instruction always begins with a period, followed by two upper case letters. Here are some examples of instructions without argument

.FS Footnote Starts
.FE Footnote Ends
.ND No Date
.TL TitLe (centred)
.PP start ParagraPh

The instructions **.FS** and **.FE** are placed respectively in front of and after the lines that are required to be printed at the foot of the page.

.ND prevents the date from being printed at the foot of each page. Under the macro option **–ms**, the date is included as a rule.

.TL automatically prints the title, centred, with five lines space before and five lines space after. This is equivalent to the following sequence of ordinary instructions.

.sp 5
.ce 1
.sp 5

The **LL** and **PO** instructions require a numerical value. This is provided using the ordinary instruction **nr**, as follows

.nr LL 40n   = line length, 40 characters
.nr PO 10n   = left margin, 10 characters

If you want to avoid complications, **LL** and **PO** are best left at their standard default values.

We shall now try another text example.

$ ex myfriendmike
"myfriendmike" [New file]
:a
.pl 40
.nr LL 40n
.ND
.TL
SUMMER EVENING IN NEW YORK

```
.PP
.NH
A cool wind blew across Manhattan
driving away the heat of the day.
We waited for the start of the concert
in a small square,
not far from Greenwich Village.
My friend said to me:
"Would you like some ice cream?
My wife and I love it."
Then all three of us began to
discuss Mozart and his music.
A few minutes later, Mike (*)
.FS                                   = start of footnote
* Author of 'nroff'
.FE                                   = end of footnote
wiped his chocolate-covered
mouth with his tie.
Until that moment, I had never
thought a tie could be used for this.
.                                     = end of text
:w                                    = save
"myfriendmike" [New file] 25 lines, 538 characters = number written
:q                                    = quit ex
$
```

We are now ready to initiate the task:

```
$ nroff -ms myfriendmike
```

           SUMMER EVENING IN NEW YORK

     A cool wind blew across Manhattan
driving away the heat of the day. We
waited the start of the concert in a
small square, not far from Greenwich
Village. My friend said to me: "Would
you like some ice cream? My wife and I
love it." Then all three of us began to
discuss Mozart and his music. A few
minutes later, Mike (*) wiped his
chocolate-covered mouth with his tie.
Until that moment, I had never thought a
tie could be used for this.

_____
* Author of 'nroff'

5.8 Escape: !
Formatting text is a repetitive task; you never get it exactly right
the first time. Generally, the **ex-nroff** sequence is repeated several
times to obtain correct result. There is a way of saving time. This
is by using the escape, symbolised by **!** under **ex.** This command
allows you to move out from the editor to the shell level and then
return back into **ex** after execution of a command(s) line. The escape
is a kind of window that allows you to communicate with the outside
world.

    To carry out an escape task, you key in the **!** followed by a line
of command(s). When the task is completed or refused for any reason,
the system sends you the **!** back.

```
$ ex myfriendmike
"myfriendmike" 25 lines, 538 characters
:! date
Sun Jul 20 16:55:23 BST 1986
!
:                                        = return to editor
```

    Similarly, you can call **nroff** from **ex**

```
! nroff -ms myfriendmike
```

    In such a case, the output is to the screen, but there is no
chance of any confusion between the text in the editor and the output from **nroff,** even though both apparently coexist on the screen.
The output from **nroff** does not remain in the editor. You are on the
same line as you were (this can be verified with **p**). If there are
any corrections to be made, you are there ready.

    As an aside, note that you can use the escape in other commands
(**mail,** cf 7.1.2).

5.9 Spelling checker: spell
This is an attractive command which checks your spelling against the
OED or Flower. Possible errors are shown on the standard output. Do
not be surprised if it contains proper names, since these do not usually appear in dictionaries. The command syntax is as follows.

```
$ spell files
```

5.10 Display control: CTRL-S CTRL-Q
When you use the display commands, the contents may not necessarily
appear on the screen if the material occupies more lines than the
display allows (usually, just over 20). You can momentarily inter-

rupt the display by CTRL-S (Stop). CTRL-Q (Quit) will provide you with the rest of the display. If you are working under UCB UNIX, the command **more** will enable you to display files, page by page, by pressing the space bar.

5.11 Summary

We have taken a general look at word processing and the text for-matters offered by UNIX.

We have become familiar with some of the ordinary **nroff** instruct-ions and used them with a short section of text.

We have also looked at the standard macro instructions **ms.**

We have then introduced the tools associated with **nroff.**

spell   spelling checker
!   escape - special command insertion

CTRL-S   stop display
CTRL-Q   quit (that is, continue display)

6 On your own

6.0 Session aim

So that you can benefit from UNIX yourself, we shall show you the on-line documentation, **man,** and the system's initiation course, **learn.**

6.1 On-line documentation: man

The commands that we reviewed in the previous five sessions are described in the UNIX Programmer's Manual. This title might appear offputting, but this book is very useful. The section of this documentation devoted to the explanation of commands (volume 1) is accessible from your terminal by keying **man** (manual). If your system is small, you may not have this feature, for reasons of space.

The command **man** takes as its argument the name of the command about which you require detailed information. We will try to obtain the description of **cat.**

```
$ man cat                           = documentation on cat, please
CAT(1)                    CAT(1)
NAME
     cat -       catenate and print
SYNOPSIS
     cat [ -u ] file ...
DESCRIPTION
     Cat  reads  each file in sequence and writes it on the standard
     output. Thus
             cat file
     prints the file, and
             cat file1 file2 > file3
     concatenates the two files and places the result on the third.
        If no input file is given,  or  if  the  argument  '-'  is
     encountered, cat reads from the standrad input file.
     Output  is  buffered  in  512-byte  blocks  unless the standard
     output is a terminal or the -u option is specified.
SEE ALSO
     pr(1), cp(1)
```

BUGS

Beware of 'cat a b >a' and 'cat a b >b', which destroy the
input files before reading them.

The first line appears with the command name followed by (1),
that is chapter 1, which corresponds to the general utility
commands, because the commands are classified in 8 categories

(1) General utility commands
(2) System calls
(3) Subroutines
(4) Special files
(5) File formats
(6) Games
(7) Languages
(8) System maintenance.

The SYNOPSIS line describes the complete syntactical form of the
command. The material enclosed in square brackets is optional; this
is where optional arguments for the command can be assigned. Of
course, the brackets themselves are not keyed in.

Note that the options are very often preceded by the less than >
symbol. On the other hand, there is no symbol in front of the
filename(s), which frees the argument order (this is why the shell
makes no distinction between 'nroff -ms untel' and 'nroff untel
-ms', for example).

Similarly, if the proposed options make a stacked list, something
like '-abcde', the specification of the options 'a' and 'e' can be
'-ae' or '-ea'.

The heading DESCRIPTION explains how the command works, especially how it behaves according to proposed options.

SEE ALSO refers you to other commands or documentation.

The heading FILES (not shown here) lists the important files that
relate to the command.

DIAGNOSTICS notes possible errors due to incorrect usage, while
BUGS indicates errors in the program.

The **man** command is useful when you know what command does what.
On the other hand, it is not so helpful when you want to know
whether there are commands to carry out such and such a function. If
you do not know the name and the contents of the command, look first
in the first part of the printed manual - the table of contents of
the permutated index. This will allow you to find a command by its
function, rather than by name.

6.2 Learn UNIX using UNIX: learn

The material explained in these first sessions belongs to the interactive course integrated within UNIX. There are six courses that can be accessed used the **learn** command, if your UNIX comprises the complete suite of courses.

```
$ learn                                 = key this name
Sorry, there is no subject or lesson to learn.
Bye
$
```

Faced with this message, there is not much you can do. The course is not available on your system. If this is not the case, your screen will display something like

```
$ learn
There are the available courses -
    C
    editor
    eqn
    files
    macros
    morefiles
```
If you want more information about the courses, or if you have never used 'learn' before, type 'return'; otherwise type the name of the course you want, followed by 'return'.

As you can see, the menu contains programming in C; the text editor, processing of mathematical formulae, eqn; an introduction to the file system; word processing with macro instructions and, finally, the file system, at a more advanced level.

After a few lines of introduction, you will be asked to press Return if this the first time that you use **learn**.

For each lesson, there is a short explanation of the subject, followed by examples. Then follows a multiple choice question; you are awarded a point for each correct answer and you move on to the next lesson.

```
.................               = the explanation continues
........                        = a question
$ answer the                    = you reply
Good  Lesson 0.1a (1)           = good, 1 mark
.....                           = next lesson
```

In lesson 0.1a the correct answer scores 1 mark. This is added to
at each correct reply.

If the reply is not acceptable, you can begin again.

```
...........
Type 'one or 'two'
$ one
$ Sorry, that's not right.
Do you want to try again? y
Try the problem again
$ two
```

After an initial incorrect response, you can still continue
further without having to reply a second time.

```
Type 'one' or 'two'
$ two
$ Sorry, that's not right.
Do you want to try again? no
OK Less 0.1f (2)
Skipping to next lesson
```

Sometimes, in order to move on to the next lesson, the system
will ask you to type 'ready'. If you want to abandon the course, you
have the special command **bye** which brings you back to the shell
level. Remember the number of the lesson that you have just
terminated so that you can continue from that point at the next
session.

When you resume the course later, instead of just pressing Return
at the beginning of the session, you will be able to specify the
course name and the number of the last lesson, each separated by a
space.

```
$ learn files 2.2a
```

Note that you will sometimes be diverted by questions peculiar to
Bell Laboratories or relating to the New Jersey area or other bits
of American culture. This course was originally developed for Bell
personnel. You may well learn something from such excursions; they
are only a minor inconvenience.

6.3 Summary
We have introduced the line documentation, **man**, and the computer-
assisted course, **learn.**

Part 2   Useful everyday commands

7   Communication facilities

7.0 Aim of session

In this session, we shall present some communication facilities, taken in a broad sense. These are reading and writing electronic mail (**mail**), opening a direct dialogue with another user (**write**), and using an electronic diary (**calendar**).

7.1 Electronic mail

7.1.1 To write

When it comes to ensuring the prompt delivery of your mail, you are never better served than by yourself! We shall therefore begin with that. First key in your login name after the command name, separated by a space. After pressing Return, that is, starting on the next line, you can type in your personal message which can run to as many lines as you like.

```
$ mail mark               = you are the destination
Subject : advert          = requests subject of 'letter'
Young man,                = start of message
smart appearance
seeks ...                 = end
EOT                       = exit via CTRL-D. Note that BSD4.2
                            indicates your typing of CTRL-D by
                            displaying EOT

$
You have mail             = mail arrives
```

As you can see, when the shell receives the CTRL-D signal, indicating the end of data from the keyboard, it knows that a letter has just been created. Use of CTRL-D is not the only way of exiting from the mail writing mode; a period at the beginning of the line produces the same effect, just as in **ex.**

The shell transmits the message 'You have mail' to the addressee, as soon as the current task is completed. In the case of **mail**, you get this message before the customary **$**, but this is an exception.

51

You can write several addressee names one after the other, separated by a space. Of course, these must be login names. If you also
include your own name along with the adressees, you can keep track
of your message.

7.1.2 To **read**

In order to read your mail, you simply key in the command **mail.** The
contents will be displayed on your screen, together with some
supplementary information, such as the name of the sender as well as
the date and time at which the message was sent.

```
$ mail                         = let's look at our mail
Mail version 2.18 5/19/83.  Type ? for help.
"/usr/spool/mail/mark": 1 message 1 new
>N  1 mark      Wed Sep  3 18:02  9/122  "advert"
& p                            = print the message
Message  1:
From mark Wed Sep   3 18:02:17 1986
To: mark
Subject: advert
Status: R
Young man,
smart appearance,
seeks...
& d                                   = delete message
& q                                   = 'quit' (or leave) the mail system
$
```

The & (ampersand) is the 'ready' symbol for the mail command; it
is asking you for a sub-command. If you key in something like Help
or ?, the system will give a list of sub-commands. They are similar
to those studied in the editor session.

q quit mail
p display contents
d destroy mail
w save mail
! escape

The command **w** (write) transfers the contents of the mail to the
file called **mbox,** in your home directory. If you specify a file
name, the mail will be transferred to it.

If you press Return (or the + key) you will normally get the next
batch of mail. Since there is none in this case, you will exit from
the mail mode by typing **q.** You will obtain the **$** prompt, indicating

that you are back with the shell. If you have several messages, **mail**
will begin by displaying the oldest and finish with the most recent.
We will try this out with two exchanges.

```
$ mail moira                    = first message
Subject: taxes 1
Meeting about taxes 1
EOT                             = End-Of-Text (CTRL-D pressed)
$ mail moira                    = second message
Subject: taxes 2
Meeting about taxes 2
EOT
You have new mail.
$
```

   Moving to read

```
$ mail
Mail version 2.18 5/19/83.  Type ? for help.
"/usr/spool/mail/moira": 2 messages 2 new
>N  1 moira      Wed Sep  3 18:11  8/144  "taxes 1"
 N  2 moira      Wed Sep  3 18:12  8/144  "taxes 2"
&
Message  1:
From moira Wed Sep  3 18:11:51 1986
Date: Wed, 3 Sep 86 19:11:43 bst
To: moira
Subject: taxes 1
Status: R

Meeting about taxes 1

&                               = Return pressed
Message  2:
From moira Wed Sep  3 18:12:08 1986
Date: Wed, 3 Sep 86 19:11:59 bst
To: moira
Subject: taxes 2
Status: R

Meeting about taxes 2
&
At EOF                          = no more letters
& q
Saved 2 messages in mbox        = messages automatically saved
$
```

7.2 Direct dialogue: **write**

Direct communication with another user is done using the command
write. This facility is intriguing for new users and necessary for
distant users requiring immediate contact. However, it is sometimes
annoying for the addressee to be disturbed in his work.

You key the command, followed by the addressee's name. You enter
your message, starting on the next line - again it can be of any
length - and terminate with CTRL-D.

```
$ write mark                          = hello Mark, this is Moira
I have done those graphics for you
EOF
$                                     = exit via CTRL-D
```

What happens at Mark's end? First, he will hear an insistent
beep; then he will see the following message.

```
Message from moira on tty02 at 18:15
I have done those graphics for you
EOF
```

The last line EOF (End Of File) corresponds to the CTRL-D that
Moira keyed immediately after her message.

This scenario assumes that both people are mutually aware that
they are each working at their terminals. In practice, it is wiser
to verify if the addressee is in fact present on the system, by using the **who** command, for example. If the person is not there, you
will receive the following message.

```
$ write alan
alan not logged in.
$
```

The system does not verify if the user (whether connected or not)
exists.

```
$ write bloggs
bloggs not logged in.
$
```

Let us return to our story. If Mark wants to converse with Moira,
he will carry out the same operation.

```
$ write moira
Many thanks
```

```
I'm coming
EOF                                      = CTRL-D pressed
$
```

If the two people wish to hold a two-way conversation, they should not use CTRL-D as that puts them back to the shell. They will need to work out a means of signalling the end of each message. Since this is just like a walkie-talkie conversation, they need an agreed means of indicating 'end of message, I'm listening'.

```
$ write mark                             = Moira speaks to Mark
This is me again Mark
Shall we have lunch at Nino's?
(Suggest 'e' for end of message)
```

    Mark reads

```
Message from moira on tty02 at 18:16
This is me again Mark.
Shall we have lunch at Nino's?
(Suggest 'e' for end of message)
```

```
$ write moira                            = Mark replies
Yes Moira, but what's on the menu?
e
```

```
Message from mark on tty03 at 18:17
Yes Moira, but what's on the menu?       = Moira reads
e

Grilled chops...                         = and replies
e

Grilled chops...                         = Mark reads
e

Fine, Moira, see you soon                = and replies
EOT
$

Fine, Moira, see you soon
EOT

EOT                                      = Moira terminates her end
                                           of the conversation

$
```

7.3 Direct communication control: mesg

When you are engaged in some work that requires your full con-
centration; for example, when writing text, you can prevent any int-
erruptions by making use of the command **mesg**.

```
$ mesg n                              = no to any messages
$
```

In this way, you can prevent all your friends from writing to you
while you are busy. Anyone trying to contact you will receive the
following message.

```
$ write mark
Permission denied
$
```

To reopen direct communication, you simply change the n to y
(yes).

```
$ mesg y                              = line reconnnected
$
```

In any event, when you leave the terminal with CTRL-D, the system
reconnects this link. You can also check the status of **mesg** at any
time with the following.

```
$ mesg
is y
$
```

7.4 Electronic diary: calendar

While it is certainly useful to be able to send mail to oneself as a
reminder, this kind of memo has its limitations. The command
calendar is more suitable; it operates as an electronic diary to
remind you of meetings, anniversaries, etc. Of course, you need to
provide the basic information for the command to be able to provide
it for you at the right time. **calendar** finds this information that
you create for it under the same name in your home directory. For
this command to function, the information file must be located in
the directory where the command is to be used. Here is an example.

```
$ cat > calendar                      = create diary
Sep 4 : Jazz concert with Daniel; 8pm Horticultural Hall
9/5 : See optician                    = 5/9 in Britain
9/6 : Yoga class                      = 6/9 in Britain
$                                     = exit with CTRL-D
```

The **calendar** file is ready. First check the date before initiating the command.   /

```
$ date
Thu Sep  4 09:11:25 BST 1986
$
```

The date is correct. Continue.

```
$ calendar                              = call the program
Sep 4 : Jazz concert with Daniel; 8pm Horticultural Hall
9/5 : See optician
$
```

Called by the shell, the calendar **command** has fetched the
calendar file (the data) that it opened and has selected from it the
information for today and tomorrow. Note that the line relating to
the day after tomorrow is not displayed. Where a Friday is involved,
the next day is understood to be the following Monday.

This command is not very flexible when it comes to reading dates.
You have to key in the first three letters of the month, followed by
the day, separated by a space. It is exactly the same as in the reply to the command **date.**

The system accepts April 20, april 20, Apr 20, apr 20, but
rejects Apr20 (no space).

You can also indicate the date in numerals only, in the same
order, but using a slash to separate the month and day.

The system will accept 09/24, 9/25. It rejects 09 24 (wrong
separator), 9-24 (wrong separator), 25/9 (incorrect order).

7.5 Calendar: cal
A calendar is sometimes useful to establish a diary in the **calendar**
file. The command **cal** will display your choice of calendar. You specify the month and year.

```
$ cal 8 86
   August 86
 S  M Tu  W Th  F  S
          1  2  3  4  5
 6  7  8  9 10 11 12
13 14 15 16 17 18 19
20 21 22 23 24 25 26
27 28 29 30 31

$
```

If this does not appear correct to you, there is a good reason.
This is the month of August of the year 0086 and not 1986. This
program covers the years from 1 to 9999! It is optional whether you
specify a particular month or not; if not mentioned, the calendar
for the complete year will be presented.

7.6 Summary
You now know the commands that are used for direct or indirect communication.

mail	read mail
	sub-commands
	d destroy mail
	p display mail
	q quit mail
	w save mail
	! diversion
mail name(s)	send a message
	end of message: period at beginning of line
write name	begin dialogue with a user
	CTRL-D to leave command
mesg	permission for direct messages
	n (no), **y** (yes)
calendar	create a diary
	data file: calendar
cal	display the calendar

8 In the interests of security

8.0 Session aim
We shall study the problem of security. We shall see how to change your password, and how to lock or unlock a file.

8.1 Changing your password: passwd
As promised in session 1, we will now look at the possibility of changing your password. When you call the command **passwd**, you initiate the following dialogue with the system.

```
$ passwd
Changing password for moira
Old password:                          = current password
New password:                          = new password
Retype new password:                   = type it again
$
```

The new password is requested again as confirmation. Be careful not to make a mistake as the echo will be cut. If the two sets of keying are not identical, the change will not occur.

```
$ passwd
Changing password for moira
Old password:
New password:
Retype new password:                   = I made a mistake!
Mismatch - password unchanged
$
```

If you do not have a password and you want to create one, the question about your current password will not appear; the system will ask for the new password straight away.

The length of a password varies from system to system, but generally it must consist of a least 4 alphanumeric or 6 alphabetic characters.

If you have forgotten your current password, it is not possible to change it. The only thing you can do is to ask the super-user to take it out of service. Not something you will be very proud of, but there is no alternative. You will be able to change it subsequently.

This password is held in the file **/etc/passwd** (see the FILES heading in the reply to the command "man passwd"). You can display it with **cat**; the output will look something like this.

```
$ cat /etc/passwd                        = we want to look
moira:VHMrvgfl.RKzw:101:10::/users/moira:
stephen:cT50dQU7vSL8E:102:10::/users/stephen:
david::103:10::/users/david:              = no password
doug:EulCUymONkxyA:104:10::/users/doug:
$
```

The second field, that is, the area including the name of the home directory, is reserved for the password. You will see that yours bears absolutely no resemblance to what you have keyed. Your password is encoded by the UNIX system with 13 characters (a mixture of numbers and letters, upper and lower case). If this encoding was not there, the field would be open to jokers.

8.2 File protection

The files in a multi-user operating system are open to everyone if they are not locked. Anyone can, without your knowing, access your files; they can list, read and even alter them. It is inconceivable for the person responsible for a project that confidential information should be on view to all. On the other hand, ease of access to a set of files is desirable when a group of people are working together on a project.

Here is an example of what can occur among users

```
$ pwd
/users/moira
$ ls -l /user/mark                        = let's list the files
total 6
   -rw-r--r--  1 mark          45 Jun  4 17:17 blocknote
   -r--r--r--  1 mark         197 Apr 22 17:18 calendar
   -rw-r--r--  1 mark         112 Oct  8 17:24 photext
   -rwxr-xr-x  1 mark         312 Oct  8 17:17 prog_c
   drwxr-xr-x  1 mark        1136 Jul 20 17:31 signex
$ cat /users/mark/blocknote               = take a peek!
These are the minutes of the next meeting.
$
```

8.2.1 Permissions

In order to understand the file protection system under UNIX, we must distinguish between two concepts: permission, and ownership of files or directories. There are three types of permission/protection: read, write and search-execute, which are associated with each directory and each file. Here is their meaning

(1) Permission to read
- For a file:
  allows the contents to be displayed.
- For a directory:
  authorises the file names it contains to be listed.

(2) Permission to write
- For a file:
  allows all alteration of the contents.
- For a directory:
  allows the creation and destruction of files.

  If writing is forbidden on a directory, you may not destroy the files, but you can alter them if writing is authorised.

(3) Permission for search-execute
- For a file:
  it is necessary for commands and programs.
- For a directory:
  it allows access to it from another directory, that is, it can be mentioned in a pathway.

8.2.2 Ownership of files and directories

For the concept of ownership, UNIX distinguishes three categories of user.

(1) The true proprietor, that is, the first person to create the directory or file. In the previous example, **mark** is the owner of **blocknote**, etc.
(2) A group of users, for example, a team of associates working on a project.
(3) A third category, the public, that is, all users accessing your system.

Depending on the category of user, these permissions/protections are designated in terms of mode. The mode of a file or a directory can be verified by the command **ls -l**, as was done in the last example. We know that for a directory the first letter **d** indicates a directory, the letter **r** corresponds to the authorisation to read, **w** to write and **x** to execute. The group 'rwx' on the left concerns the true proprietor, in this case the user **mark**; the next group of three letters represents the permissions for the user group; the last three letters refer to permissions for everyone else.

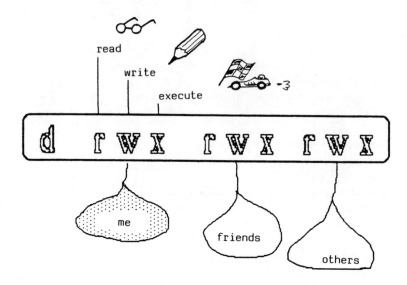

If the triplets in drwxrwxrwx are typical of a directory, those in -rw-rw-rw- are representative of an ordinary text file like blocknote. Since the file is neither a program or a command, execution is not authorised; **x** is replaced by - for the three user categories.

The drawing illustrates the permissions for a directory of which you are the owner.

8.3 Changing a file mode: chmod
You can use the command **chmod** to change the mode of a file or a directory when it is yours.

```
$ cat > remind_me                    = create a file
who are you
$                                    = end with CTRL-D
```

Let's look at the permissions granted on this file.

```
$ ls -l remind_me
-rw-rw-r--  1 jam        12 Sep  4 09:52 remind_me
$
```

To use the **chmod** command, you designate the mode, then the file(s) or directory(ies).

```
$ chmod +x remind_me
$ ls -l rem*
-rwxrwxr-x  1 jam         12 Sep  4 09:52 remind_me
$
```

This file is now executable; taken as a whole, the shell considers it to be a command. It is equivalent to giving a new name to the command **who am I**, which in this precise case is only valid in the current directory. You now only have to key **remind_me** or **who am I** to obtain your identity (cf session 4 on the shell).

8.3.1 Symbolic mode

In order to specify the argument of the mode, the following symbols are placed in front of the letters **r**, **w** or **x**.

+ add a permission
- delete a permission

If required, the argument can begin with a letter to indicate the user category.

u user (you)
g group of users
o others

You can therefore freely specify permissions according to the user category. For example, if you want to prevent others from writing, you can construct this command line.

```
$ chmod go-w remind_me
$
```

You will get an error message if you do not observe the following points.

(1) There must be no internal spacing within the argument. 'go -w' is incorrect.
(2) The file name(s) must appear after the mode.
(3) This command does not function for other people's files (unless you are the super-user).
(4) UNIX will not protect a non-existent file.

Since one can never be absolutely sure of oneself, it is advisable to protect any perfected program or section of text against any
damage or interference, by write protecting from others and even
yourself. This may appear strange, but in this way the file is
preserved from any rash use of the **rm** command. For example

```
$ cp Edinburgh Edinburgh_good
$ chmod -w Edinburgh_good
$ rm Edinburgh_good
rm: override protection 444 for Edinburgh_good? n
                              = reply y or n; if y, file destroyed
$
```

To update the version in question, we unlock the file Edin-
burgh_good, authorising write, and we copy the good version to it.
To conclude, we must relock the file.

```
$ chmod +w Edinburgh_good
$ cp Edinburgh Edinburgh_good
$ chmod -w Edinburgh_good
$
```

In fact, in order to protect a file completely, we must at the
same time

- forbid writing to the directory that contains it and
- forbid writing to the file itself.

8.3.2 Numeric mode

Certain versions of UNIX do not authorise the symbols that we have
just examined. Instead they adopt a three-digit numerical coding
(for example 755), representing from right to left: you, your group,
and the other users, according to the respective permissions
numbered as follows.

4 read authorised
2 write authorised
1 search-execute authorised
0 no authorisation

You therefore only have to remember these four numbers of the
code. The remainder, that is, the total of the permissions or prot-
ections, is arrived at by simple addition.

6 read or write authorised: 4+2 = 6
5 read or search-execute authorised: 4+1 = 5
3 write and search-execute authorised: 2+1 = 3
7 complete authorisation: 4+2+1 = 7

For example, the argument 700 means that the user alone has complete authorisation. If you are more altruistic, you will use either 744 or 644 which authorise at least the display or listing of a file. Here are two other examples of how the coding is used.

```
$ chmod 755 my_prog
$ chmod 644 my_text
$
```

8.4 Coding a file: crypt
For those who are obsessive about file protection, some versions of UNIX contain the command **crypt**. If you specify the password, the command reads the data on the standard input and sends it 'scrambled' to the standard output. For the password, the echo is inhibited as on login. Here is a simple test.

```
$ crypt
Enter key:
12345678
abcdefgh
                                = CTRL-D
C$dS²'Gn/!:vz                   = abracadabra
$
```

In the next example, the key moira is specified in order to code the file **clear**; the result is saved in **unclear.**

```
$ crypt moira < clear > unclear
$ rm clear
$
```

This same command is used to code and decode a file, by specifying the same password.

```
$ crypt moira < unclear > light
$
```

Note that coding of the file is also possible under **ed** with the command **x.**

8.5 Summary
The following commands concerned with the protection of files have been presented.

passwd to change the password
chmod   to change the file mode
           symbolic arguments:
           + add a permission
           - delete a permission
           r read
           w write
           x execute
           u user
           g group of users
           o other users

           4 permission to read
           2 permission to write
           1 permission to search/execute
           0 no authorisation
crypt   (key) to code a file

9 Execution

9.0 Session aim

We shall now concern ourselves with the different methods of initiating the execution of commands. We shall first study the **pipe**, which allows commands to be connected one to another; then we shall look at the commands that relate to the execution of a background task.

9.1 Pipe

We touched upon the connection of commands by **pipe** in session 2. There, we simply stated that the standard output of a command can serve as the standard input of another command. In fact, the UNIX system reserves memory space for this operation which acts as a communication buffer between the two commands. This novel linking **pipe** concept is a feature that other operating systems have now adopted.

This chaining is symbolised by a vertical bar, shown on most terminal displays as two vertical dashes, one above the other. If you use this symbol between commands on the same line, you are requesting the shell to set up a connection between these commands. A line of commands chained by **pipe** is called a **pipeline**. Space before and after this symbol is optional.

```
$ ls -l | wc -l
       5                              = reply
$
```

Here we asked for a detailed list of the files (**ls -l**) and the output is sent to the command **wc** which counts the number of lines (**wc -l**). Before embarking on a detailed explanation of this command (session 10), we will mention here that we obtain the number of files and sub-directories that are at present in the current directory.

Several commands can be linked with the vertical symbol. For example, we will send the number 5 to the printer with the command **lpr** (examined later).

```
$ ls -l | wc -l | lpr          = print
$                              = awaiting the output
```

We could have obtained the same result with sequential instructions using a temporary file, but in a much less elegant way. First, management of provisional files is left to you; this is certainly not the case with pipelines. What is more, it is quicker: the two commands are executed simultaneously and there is a good chance that they will intercommunicate without accessing the disk. This would not be so if we followed this procedure:

```
$ ls -l > provisionall
$ wc -l < provisionall > provisional2
$ lpr provisional2             = wait for file to be printed; then
$ rm provisional?              = destroy files
$
```

9.2 Filter

We cannot form a pipeline with just any command. At the head of a pipeline, the command must write the result on the standard output. At the end, it must read the data on the standard input. The intermediate position, that is, the area between the two vertical bars, must contain a command that uses both the standard input and the standard output.

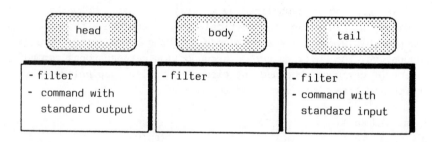

This final category of command is called the **filter.** This carries out some operation on the input and places the result at the output.

To be precise, the filter operates for as long as there is something on its standard input (for as long as the water is poured, to adopt the metaphor of the following example).

```
kettle | coffee-filter | coffee-jug
```

The commands of a pipeline can for example be in the initial position: **echo, who, who am I, ls,** etc. They take their data from

somewhere other than the standard input, but they at least use the
standard output.

In chaining, commands of the filter type, like **cat, rev, nroff,**
wc can be located in any position, whether at the head, in the
middle, or at the end. In subsequent sessions, you will   meet other
filters: **pr, sort, uniq, grep, tr, sed, tail,** etc.

The typical case of the end of a pipeline is the command **lpr**
which activates the printer, or the directing of the output to a
file.

$ who **|** wc > file

On the other hand, redirection of the standard input is only done
by a filter in the initial position.

$ rev < file **|** sort   ...

9.3 Collect intermediate results: tee
With the pipe, the intermediate results of course do not appear on
the screen, and we do not need to know them. But if you really want
to know them, insert the command **tee** (T) in the pipeline, as below.

$ who **|** tee /dev/tty **|** wc -l   = /dev/tty designates your terminal

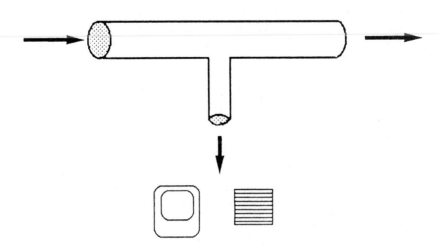

You will see the output of **who** on the screen, then that of **wc.**
Then if you want to save these intermediate results in a file, give
it a name after **tee.**

```
$ who | tee whoarethere | wc
```

9.4 Linking commands
We will study this example.

```
$ pwd
/users/mark
$ (cd /dev ; ls)
tty02
ttyh0
ttyhl
console
printer
$ pwd
/users/mark
$
```

The shell has accessed directory **/dev** (without handing you back control) in order to list the files that are there; then it has returned to the current directory. The set of commands in brackets is considered by the shell to be a single command. This linking of commands can also have its inputs and outputs redirected.

```
$ (cd ; pwd ; ls -l) | lpr
```

Here, the output of the three commands is connected to **lpr** to be printed out on the same page. On the other hand, if we were to pro-ceed as below, the output of each command would be printed on a different sheet.

```
$ cd | lpr; pwd | lpr : ls -l | lpr
```

9.5 Process
At the beginning of this book, we explained that UNIX was developed for simultaneous operations (multi-tasking and multi-users). This means that, at any time, users can undertake several tasks at the same time. Each task initiated is called a process in UNIX termin-ology.

9.5.1 Process in the foreground
When you login, a process (the shell) is created to maintain a dialogue with you at the terminal. Each time you send a command, the shell initiates the corresponding process. Being created in con-versational mode, this is termed a foreground process, because it

happens in front of you. The commands that we have experimented with up until now are good examples of this.

9.5.2 Initiating a background task: &

The above is in contrast to the background process. You will have seen that a program can function for a long time without asking you for anything, before handing you back control. For example, if you send a long file to **nroff**, you must wait quite a long time to obtain the shell prompt that indicates the end of the task. To avoid this wait, you can ask the shell to execute the program in the background.

All you need to do is to add the **&** (ampersand) symbol to the end of the command line. Spaces are optional.

```
$ nroff -ms roman &            = a little while later you get ...
10261
$
```

This command line will be executed offstage. The shell will give you the **$**, without keeping you waiting long, just the time it takes to give you a number. This number is called the process identity number, assigned to the activated command (here **nroff**). Note this PID (Process IDentity), because you will need to use it if you want to cancel the task before it is completed. As soon as you have the prompt on your screen, you can proceed to another task. In this situation, you are in the position of being able to execute two tasks in parallel. You can even logout, leaving the background process to carry on.

Note, though, that if you have not taken the precaution to work in the background, you will not be able to logout without interrupting everything. In fact, to be logged out, you have to have the **$** prompt; and this can only be obtained by pressing the CTRL-C key, which itself means abandoning the task. A Catch 22 situation!

The **nroff** output in the above example will interrupt our foreground work, because of the way the command line is structured it uses the standard output. The two outputs will be mixed. The first solution is to save the output of the background process to a file.

```
$ nroff -ms roman > gropave &
10262
$
```

The **&** does not have to be placed at the end of a command line.

```
$ job1 & job2
```

The first task will be executed in the background and the second
in the foreground. You will be handed back control at the end of
job2. On the other hand, if the ampersand is placed at the end of
line as well, you will be handed back control immediately.

```
$ jobl & job3 &
10265
10266
$
```

A task can be a set of commands linked between brackets.

```
$ (nroff -ms roman | wc ; rev < dico | sort) &
10267
$
```

9.6 Interrogating process status: ps
You may well want to know at some point what stage your background
task has reached. The **ps** (Process Status) command allows you to interrogate the computer about this. The command name may be different
on your system. In any case, the **ps** command without option will
display lines of this kind.

```
$ ps
  PID TTY TIME COMMAND
 5181 02  0:17 -sh
 6952 02  0:04 ps
$
```

Several items of information are included in the command reply.
First, the numbers 5181 and 6952: these are the identity numbers of
processes being handled when this command line was initiated. This
number represents the numerical order of the processes initiated by
users since the start of the day. The first is the shell (**-sh**)
initiated when you logged in; the second is the process **ps** that the
shell initiated itself. Also shown are the terminal (TTY), the time
used by the machine and finally the command names (COMMAND). Some
versions of **ps** give fuller information; for example, the status of
your process, whether it is currently running or has been suspended.

```
$ nroff -ms Edinburgh > kir&
10271
$ ps
  PID TTY STAT  TIME COMMAND
10242 02  S     0:02 -sh
```

```
10271 02  R      0:02 nroff -ms Edinburgh
10272 02  R      0:00 ps
$
```

We   have   used   the **ps** command immediately after the text processing. If the next interrogation using **ps** no longer displays the process name, the task in question is completed, or has been abandoned if there was an anomaly.

9.7 Abandon background proces: kill
If for some reason the initiated background task has to be interrupted, it is necessary to send the PID number to the command **kill**. If you wanted to stop the background task whose PID number you have noted, you simply do the following.

```
$ kill 6989
$
```

If this interrupted process called other sub-processes, they will also be killed. Of course, you cannot kill tasks that are already completed or that have been deleted.

```
$ kill 6989
6989: No such process
$
```

9.8 Yielding priority: nice
It is clear that the more work that there is to be done, the more execution in the computer will be slowed, because the machine's capacity is sliced up like a cake. So, the act of initiating several huge tasks in the background is not very kind to others. If you are not in a hurry to obtain the output of a task, you can send it to the background with a qualified priority. You just need the command **nice.**

```
$ nice nroff -ms myfriendmike > Mike&
10276
$
```

9.9 Summary
We have introduced in this session the connecting of commands called the pipeline.

- a pipeline is made up of pipes and filters
- the pipe is symbolised by a vertical bar
- the filter is a command that has standard input and output
- the head and the tail of a pipeline can be other than of filter
  type
- the **tee** command allows intermediate results to be recovered.

You have learnt about the linking of commands:

(line of commands)

We have distinguished between:

- foreground process, and
- background process (commands followed by **&**)

The commands that are useful for initiating a background task
are:

ps   interrogates process status (displays PID number)
kill PID   abandon background process
nice   priority control.

10 Manipulating text files

In the next two sessions we shall do a tour of the commands that
serve to manipulate files that contain textual data.

We shall study the output of a file to a printer, preparation of
the output, the sort, and finally counting the elements in a file.

10.1 Output to a printer: lpr
Output on paper (hard copy) can be obtained by using the command
cat, together with redirection to the terminal allocated for this
task. The command line will look something like the following.

```
$ cat myfriendmike > /dev/tty09           = fictitious example
```

Here, the directory **/dev** (device) contains the files of those
terminals that have names beginning with tty (special files). In our
example, **tty09** is a special file for the printer terminal. Causing
the **cat** command to function redirecting the output to this special
file should theoretically cause the result to be displayed on the
terminal assigned to this special file; that is, it should print it.

But if it so happens that this terminal is already occupied, you
will not get the expected output. To avoid this source of annoyance,
there is a program called **spooler** which permits a printer to be controlled. The word derives from Simultaneous Peripheral Output On-
Line. Under UNIX, the spooler is called **lpr** (line printer) in most
cases; this can easily be checked with the supervisor. We shall try
the following command.

```
$ nroff -ms Edinburgh > Scotland
$ lpr Scotland
$
```

Or, using a pipe

```
$ nroff -ms Edinburgh | lpr
$
```

When this command is accepted by the shell, you will receive the $ prompt almost immediately. However, this does not mean that your output is ready. As is often the case, you have to get into line and wait your turn. When the printer is available, the 'demon' will awaken and way his magic wand for the output. A program like the spooler, which comes into operation when necessary, is called a 'demon', a term first introduced by specialists in the field of AI. The electronic mailman who sends the message 'You have mail' as soon as a letter is created alongs belongs to this category of demonic command.

The **-m** option is a useful means of being warned by a message. This avoids your having to go back and forth between your terminal and the printer; while waiting, you can do something else.

```
$ nroff -ms Edinburgh | lpr -m &
1823
$ .....                                  = another job
You have mail
$
```

10.2 Preparing a file to print: pr

Apart from the text formatted by **nroff**, output with **lpr** is not very well presented. This is because the flow of data is not divided up according to the length of the page. This is why we usually use **pr** (prepare) in order to format the output of a file, before sending it to **lpr** via a pipe.

```
$ pr epistol | lpr -m
$
```

This command has a rich range of options, almost twenty. We shall look at a few of them. First, and not optional, there will be a heading line that includes the date, the name of the file and the page number; there will also be some blank lines at the head and the foot of the page. Here is a small example.

```
$ pr Shakespeare_plays
```

                                        = start of display

Sep 5 09:22 1986 Shakespeare_plays Page 1

```
Julius Caesar          : 1950
Antony and Cleopatra : 1951
Othello                : 1956
```

The heading and margins can be deleted with the option **-t**, which also removes blank lines at the top of the page.

The option **-h** (header) followed by a string of characters in double quotes will be printed in place of the file name.

```
$ pr -h "==== Shakespeare ====" Shakespeare_*
```

```
Sep  5 09:22 1986  ==== Shakespeare ==== Page 1
```

```
Julius Caesar          : 1950
Antony and Cleopatra : 1951
Othello                : 1956
```

You can alter the length and width of the output page. Option **-w** (width) allows you to alter the standard 72 characters per line (letter width) to the value of your choice, say to '-wl32' which is the width of normal printout paper.

On the other hand, it is not advisable to change the page length. If this is not done with great care, the output will be offset.

For a large file, it is sensible to print it out in two columns, using the maximum page width, with '-2' (-3 for three columns). These two options will require a command line as follows.

```
$ pr -2 -wl32 large_file | lpr
```

10.3 Sorting procedure: sort

UNIX also provides a sorting utility program, **sort.** This command reads the data that is normally found in a sort file (by default, the keyboard), and sends the results to the standard output. First, we will set up a small file, to which we will apply the command.

```
$ cat > Shakespeare
Cassio   John Gielgud
Antony   Laurence Olivier
Iago     Richard Burton
$                              = end of file CTRL-D
```

If we sort this file, the result displayed on the screen will be:

```
$ sort Shakespeare
Antony  Laurence Olivier
Cassio  John Gielgud
Iago    Richard Burton                = look at the first character
$
```

Sort has made an alphabetical sort with reference to the first column. To obtain a sorted list of the actors (second column), a field has to be skipped, namely the first, containing the names of characters. To specify the skip accurately, the + symbol is used, followed by the number of fields to be skipped. A field is designated implicitly by a space (blank or tab).

```
$ sort +1 Shakespeare
Antony  Laurence Olivier
Cassio  John Gielgud
Iago    Richard Burton
$
```

On some systems, the output will not be correct. Why? The first space after the play character being taken to be the field separator, the second field begins with a space instead of a letter. To ensure that sort ignores insignificant spaces, you need to use the option **–b.**

```
$ sort -b +1 Shakespeare
Cassio  John Gielgud
Antony  Laurence Olivier
Iago    Richard Burton
$
```

Let us now alter our list of plays in order to obtain a sort in descending order.

```
$ echo "Merchant of Venice   : 1952" >> Shakespeare_plays
$ cat Shakespeare_plays
Julius Caesar        : 1950
Antony and Cleopatra : 1951
Othello              : 1956
Merchant of Venice   : 1952
$
```

This operation implies three additional options. We have just used the colon : as a field separator. We therefore need to inform **sort** of this character separator after **-t** (tabulation). Thus, in this case -t:. In this way, the spaces and tabulations will not be taken to be separators. The first part of the command line will thus be

sort -t:

Since we are interested in the year, **sort** must ignore the first field by skipping it, thus

sort -t: +1

We must also add the option **r** (reverse) in order to invert the classification in the years column. This gives

sort -rt: +1

Finally, the **n** option indicates that the numeric sort is required for the year sort.

```
$ sort -nrt: +1 Shakespeare_plays
Othello                : 1956
Merchant of Venice     : 1952
Antony and Cleopatra : 1951
Julius Caesar          : 1950
$
```

10.4 Deleting identical lines: uniq

After sorting a file with **sort,** you will sometimes find consecutive identical lines. If your **sort** is provided with the option that allows you to retain only the first occurrence (**-u**), you can avoid this happening. If your **sort** does not include such an option, the operation can be carried out via a pipe that will connect the commands **sort** and **uniq.**

```
$ sort file | uniq > file/sort
```

10.5 Counting: wc

The command **wc** (word count) will count the number of lines, words and characters in a file.

```
$ wc Shakespeare
        3         9          70 Shakespeare
$ wc < Shakespeare
        3         9          70
$
```

The figures in the reply correspond, respectively and in order, to the number of lines, words and characters. For **wc** a word is taken to be every sequence of characters separated by a space or a Return. The number of characters also includes Return. Note that for every redirected input, **wc** no longer displays the file name.

If we are only interested in the number of lines, the option **-l** will give us what we want. Options **-w** and **-c** are used to obtain the number of words and characters. The default option is '-lwc'.

```
$ wc -l Shakespeare*
        3 Shakespeare
        4 Shakespeare_plays
        7 total
$
```

We have just counted the lines in the **Shakespeare** and **Shakespeare_plays** files. The file names have been sent to the shell with the asterisk metacharacter. We could have keyed 'wc -l Shakespeare Shakespeare_plays'.

As a bonus, here is an example of a pipe to find out how many colleagues are working at the computer.

```
$ who | wc -l
        8
$
```

10.6 Summary
You will certainly have gained some idea of the tools required for manipulating textual data. Here are the commands, with some of their options.

lpr   output to a printer
            -m provides an end of task message

pr   prepare a file to print
            -t delete margins
            -h insert heading
            -wn width of n chararacters
            -n output in n columns

sort   sort program
             +n skip n fields
             -b ignore spaces
             -t field separator (example -t:)
             -r inverted sort
             -n numeric sort
             -u unique output

uniq   inhibit identical consecutive lines in a file

wc   count
             -l lines
             -w words
             -c characters

11 Strings

11.0 Session aim

We shall first consider the commands that let you compare files. We then introduce the command **grep**, that searches for a string, and the command **tr** that transposes characters, with a view to extending our knowledge of the metacharacters.

11.1 Comparing files

UNIX provides commands to allow you to make comparisons between two given files. These commands are **cmp** (CoMParison), **comm** (COMMon) and **diff** (DIFFerence), which at first glance might appear redundant, but which are in fact complementary. In all cases, only quite subtle comparisons will have any meaning, for example, between versions that come from the same source.

11.2 Comparing two files: cmp

The command **cmp** compares two files given as arguments, by looking line by line, byte by byte (character by character) to find the differences. The command will tell you the line number and the number of characters that are different. No message indicates that no difference has been found.

```
$ cat  Shakespeare             = remind ourselves of the file's
                                 contents
Antony  Laurence Olivier
Cassio  John Gielgud
Shylock Michael Redgrave
Iago    Richard Burton
$ cp Shakespeare William       = let's make a copy
$ cmp Shakespeare William      = compare them
$                              = no difference
```

   If we alter these files a bit.

```
$ echo "Anthony Grimble" >> Shakespeare      = add this
$ echo "Christopher Bloggs" >> William       = add that
$
```

We   now   compare them to obtain a meaningful response to the command.

```
$ cmp William Shakespeare
William Shakespeare differ: char 96, line 5
$
```

11.3 Find identical lines in two files: comm
When you want the common part of two files that have been previously
sorted, you can use the comm command. We shall create two small
files, each of three lines, and examine them with comm.

```
$ cat newcar
R11
R14
R25
$
$ cat second_hand_car
R14
R15
R16
$
```

We try the command.

```
$ comm newcar second_hand_car
R11
                R14
        R15
        R16
R25
$
```

```
File1  File2   Common
```

The comm command replies in three columns
- the first relates only to the lines contained the first file;
- the second, the lines contained in the second file;
- the third contains the lines common to both files.

You may delete some columns from the reply by inserting the
appropriate option. If you only want the common lines, you need to
delete the first and second columns. This command for this will be
as follows.

```
$ comm -12 newcar second_hand_car
R14
$
```

   To see the effect of the line order, we will sort **second_hand_car** into inverse alphabetical order.

```
$ sort -r second_hand_car > second_hand_car2        = inverse sort
$ cat second_hand_car2
R16
R15
R14
$
```

   Result of the comparison

```
$ comm -12 second_hand_car second_hand_car2
R16
$
```

   Because the comparison is carried out line by line, the line order is of paramount importance.

11.4 Find **the** differences between **two** files: **diff**

The command **diff** indicates those lines that differentiate two files. Using our previous example, we will create a slightly different version using the text editor.

```
$ cat second_hand_car3
R14
R15
R16 TX
$
```

   We now try the effect of **diff** on these two files.

```
$ diff second_hand_car second_hand_car3
3c3
< R16
---
> R16 TX
$
```

   The first line of the reply '3c3' means that line 3 has been changed (c). The contents of line 3 of the first file **second_**

hand_car is preceded by the < symbol; the same line of the second file appears after the > symbol. To appreciate the correspondence between symbols and files, imagine a parenthesis '<>'; the first file in the command line corresponds to the first element in this parenthesis.

Instead of '3c3', you would get '3d3' if that line had been destroyed in one of the files. Similarly, the letter **a** will appear if a new line has been added.

It may happen that two apparently identical files will be judged to be different, because of space characters.

```
$ cat > stars_1
heavenly bodies
$                         = CTRL-D
$ cat > stars_2
heavenly     bodies
$                         = CTRL-D
$ diff stars_1 stars_2
1c1
< heavenly bodies
---
> heavenly     bodies
$
```

You can use the option **-b** (blank) which ignores spaces.

```
$ diff -b stars??
$
```

11.5 Find lines in a file: grep
The command **grep** is a utility program that looks for a specified string in one or more files. The lines that contain this string will be displayed at the standard output.

grep derives from the text editor syntax. It searches Globally for a Regular Expression and Prints it on the screen.

g/**r**egular-**e**xpression/**p**

We will start with a simple example. Suppose we want to find the 1952 Shakespeare production from our **Shakespeare_plays** file.

```
$ cat Shakespeare_plays        = remind ourselves of the file's
Julius Caesar          : 1950     contents
Antony and Cleopatra   : 1951
```

```
The Merchant of Venice   : 1952
Othello                  : 1956
$
$ grep "1952" Shakespeare_plays
The Merchant of Venice   : 1952      = system's reply
$
```

As you can see, the first argument of the command is the target string; the command only accepts one string at a time. The second argument is the file name or the list of file names. If there is any doubt about the file name (say between **Shakespeare** and **Shakespeare_plays**), we can rely on the expansion capacity of the shell's metacharacters. Here is another example.

```
$ grep "R16" second*
second_hand_car:R16
second_hand_car2:R16
second_hand_car3:R16 TX
$
```

The command has found two lines containing the specified string, in three different files.

If the string contains spaces, it must be placed within single or double quotes. It is advisable to get into the habit of using them anyway, to avoid some unexpected surprises.

```
$ grep R16 TX second*
TX: No such file or directory
$
```

In this example, the characters 'TX' have been taken to be the file name, which the shell was unable to find. This emphasises the importance of delimiting the target string.

The option **-v** lets you invert the function of the **grep** command, that is, it extracts all lines except those you seek. This has the effect of deleting all the lines that contain the expression specified as the argument in the command line.

```
$ cat Shakespeare                        ·= look at this file
Antony  Laurence Olivier
Cassio  John Gielgud
Shylock Michael Redgrave
Iago    Richard Burton
$
```

And if the **-v** is inserted

```
$ grep -v "Antony" Shakespeare
Cassio   John Gielgud
Shylock Michael Redgrave
Iago     Richard Burton
$
```

As an exercise, think what result you would obtain with the following command line.

```
$ grep "R11" newcar | grep -v "R14"
```

Solution:.nevele R s'tI

11.6 grep's special characters
We shall now see how to use a target expression made up of special (meta)characters. In this context, because we are working according to rules relating to special characters in order to create a target string, we use the term **regular expression**.

(1) Caret and dollar
The caret and dollar characters represent the beginning and ends of lines, respectively.

```
$ grep "^Antony" Shakespeare
Antony  Laurence Olivier
$ grep "1956$" Shakespeare_plays
Othello                  : 1956          = system's response
$
```

(2) Period
The period stands for any single character (letter, digit, symbol). For example, '.z.' represents a sequence of three characters, the second of which is z.

(3) Asterisk
The asterisk represents any number of repeats of the preceding character; this number can be zero. For example

'br*' can stand for 'b', 'br','brrrrr'.

Often, the period and asterisk are used together to designate a string of any characters of any length.

```
$ grep "^The.*52" Shakespeare_plays
The Merchant of Venice   : 1952          = system's reply
$
```

In this example, the system looks for a line beginning with T and ending with 2; everything else between these characters is represented by '.*'.

A note of warning: do not confuse special characters at the shell level with those that are used in **grep**. Remember that for the shell, in file names, **?** stands for any single character, while ***** stands for any sequence of characters. The **grep** special characters are valid for the **ed** and **sed** editors (cf sessions 13.2 and 13.4).

(4) Square brackets

Square brackets are used to refer to a single character in a list whose elements are placed within square brackets. Thus, the regular expression "[Vv][Oo]" gives four different combinations: 'VO', 'Vo', 'vO' and 'vo'.

(5) Hyphen or dash

The hyphen indicates a range, from one element to another, if it constitutes a sequence of increasing values in the ASCII code. The latter is an abbreviation of American Standard Code for Information Interchange. You can consult the ASCII table which is held in a UNIX file by keying

```
$ cat /usr/pub/ascii
```

In this table, the numbers from 0 to 9 appear first, followed immediately by the upper case and then the lower case letters, in alphabetical order. To summarise

[0-9] designates any digit
[a-z] designates any lower case letter
[A-Z] designates any upper case letter

For example, the following regular expression

"[a-c][1-3]"

would describe the lines that contain:
  'a1','a2','a3','b1','b2','b3','c1','c2','c3'.

(6) Caret (continued)

When the caret is used within square brackets, it has another

meaning from the one described above. It indicates that the arguments that follow it are to be excluded. Here is an example.

```
$ grep "^[^AI]" Shakespeare     = exclude items beginning with A or I
Cassio   John Gielgud
Shylock Michael Redgrave
$
```

The system will search for lines that do not begin with A or I
within the named file.

(7) Backslash
When you want to cancel the interpretation of a special character or
other special symbol, you insert a backslash in front of the particular character.
    Here is an example with the **grep** command.

```
$ cat prog
a = 3.1416
b = 2.7182
c = a * b
$ grep \* prog                   = we seek an asterisk
c = a * b                        = found it
$
```

We shall examine this in closer detail in session 21.

11.7 Replace a character: tr
The command **tr** transposes characters one by one. We will start with
a very simple case - changing a lower case 'a' into upper case 'A'.

```
$ tr a A
a aa aaa bb                      = a line of data +CR
A AA AAA bb                      = reply
$                                = exit with CTRL-D
```

As you can see, **tr** reads the data at the standard input and replies to the standard output; therefore, if you want to use the files
as input/output media, you must redirect them. We will now try con-
verting from lower to upper case.

```
$ tr "[a-z]" "[A-Z]" < Shakespeare
ANTONY  LAURENCE OLIVIER
CASSIO  JOHN  GIELGUD
SHYLOCK MICHAEL REDGRAVE
```

IAGO   RICHARD BURTON
$

   We studied the use of the square brackets and hyphen special
characters above, with the **grep** command. Here, the operation works
in this way: the **tr** command reads the data, character by character.
If an item coincides with an element in the input list 'a-z', the
command replaces it with the corresponding character taken from the
output list 'A-Z'.
   You can play a trick on your friends with **tr** by altering the keys
of a terminal; if you key 'a', 'b' will be displayed; for 'b', a 'c'
appears, etc.

```
$ tr "[a-y]" "[b-x]"
abc                                = the original
bcd                                = the translation
$
```

   You have just checked that the command functions as planned.
Clear the screen, and ask a friend to key in a message...
   Option **-s** (stack) condenses a sequence of identical characters
into one. It is useful for eliminating spaces.

```
$ tr -s " " " " < Shakespeare_plays
Julius Caesar : 1950
Antony and Cleopatra : 1951
The Merchant of Venice : 1952
Othello : 1956
$
```

   Every line, whether filled or blank, is always terminated with
Return, and if there is a blank line, there are two successive
Returns. Empty lines could also be eliminated by stacking useless
Returns. Here, you use the ASCII code " 012" for Return.

```
$ cat lines                        = original file
111

                                   = empty line
2222

33333
$
$ tr -s "\012" "\012" < lines      = gives
111
```

```
2222
33333
$
```

Here is another example of **tr** in a pipeline. You want to know the list of different words contained in a file that we shall call **addenda**.

```
$ tr " " "\012" < addenda | sort | uniq
```

Here is how the operation works:
- spaces between words are converted into Returns, giving one word per line
- sort of the standard output from tr
- deletion of successive identical lines.

11.8 Summary
You have tried out the following commands.

cmp	compare files
comm	find common part of files
	-n deletes n columns at the output (n=1,2,3)
diff	detects differences between files
	-b ignores spaces in the comparison
grep	find lines in a file
	-v inverts command function
tr	replace one character with another
	-s shrinks a sequence of identical characters into one.

You have also become familiar with the following metacharacters.

Symbol	Meaning	Example	Commentary
^	start of line	^The	'The' at start of line
[^]	exclude	[^a]	no 'a'
$	end of line	9$	9 at line end
.	a character	...	3 characters
*	repeat	.*	sequence of characters
[]	element of	[abc]	one letter in 'abc'
-	range	[a-b]	one letter in 'abc'
\	cancel	*	symbol in place of

Part 3   Editing text

12   Further into ex

12.0 Session aim
We return to **ex**. We shall look more closely at line addressing, and
apply it to the commands already introduced in session 4. To
conclude, we shall examine some new basic commands.

12.1 Number of current line
At any time, you can obtain the number of the current line by keying
.=. The period indicates the current line when it is used in the
specification of the address, and the equals sign causes the line
number to be displayed.

```
.=                                      = where am I?
12                                      = at line 12
```

    The = symbol can also function with $, to indicate the last line
of text in the buffer memory.

```
$=                                      = what is the total?
87
```

12.2 Line addressing

12.2.1 By line number
We know how to shift the line pointer, by specifying the required
line number. But it must be accepted that this method becomes less
useful when, during the course of our work, we have had to add or
delete lines.

```
2d                                      = line 2 destroyed
```

    So, after deleting line 2, the former line 3 becomes line 2. In a
large file containing several hundred lines, counting the lines
visually does not really conform to our image of information

technology. To solve this problem, we outlined in session 4 an empirical method which involves displaying a line located above the target and then descending by pressing Return.

12.2.2 By **plus or minus**
We can get an identical result by using the + sign followed by Return.

```
+                                    = go to next line
```

This is equivalent to a simple Return, which is not especially interesting in itself. This sign can be repeated several times; to move on 9 lines, we can key + nine times, or more economically

```
+9                                    = less tiring
or
.+9
```

but here the period is superfluous. It would, however, be indispensable if in an address a comma had been chosen as the separator.

Sometimes, you go past a selected line by mistake. To go back, you need to use the - sign, followed by Return. This symbol can also be repeated or combined with a numerical argument.

```
-                                    = go back one line
---                                  = go back 3
-9                                   = go back 9
$-1                                  = to penultimate line
```

12.2.3 By **context**
To find a line by its context, let us write a few lines.

```
a                                    = write mode
There was an old woman
Who swallowed a fly.
I wonder why
She swallowed that fly.
Perhaps she'll die.
.                                    = end of text
:
```

If we now look for a line.

```
:/was  an/                          = 2 spaces
Pattern not found                   = can't find
:/was an/
There was an old woman              = found
```

You can also include +, -, or = to assist your search by context.

```
:/was an/=                          = number?
1
```

After this search, the pointer is on line 1, which becomes the current line. From which

```
:.+2                                = display
I wonder why
```

You can also use the + and - signs by themselves, or followed by a number.

```
:/wonder/-
Who swallowed a fly
```

The instruction given above has displayed the line before the one containing the word 'wonder'. Here is another example in the same vein.

```
:/a fly/+3
Perhaps she'll die.
```

12.2.4 Accessing lines
In order to display the complete contents of the buffer memory, we have learnt to write

```
1,$p                                = display everything
```

Again, in order to destroy a number of lines with the command **d**, we have used the same method of line access (addressing in terms of ex).

```
2,4d
```

We can replace these numbers by all that we have just learned. If we want to display two lines before and after the current line, we need to key

.-2,.+2p

   Similarly, with context referencing, the instruction

/fly/-,$p

will display the text from the line located above the one containing
'fly', to the end.
   Note that the first element of the address must be below the
second; '19,2p', for example, will give an error message.

12.3 Revision of some commands

12.3.1 Command e (continued)
We have learnt two ways of specifying a file; either on the command
line calling **ex** itself, or with the **e** command, after entering **ex**.
   If you give a file name that you have created and **ex** responds
"New file" or "No such file or directory", there are several possible reasons for this. There may be an error in keying the file
name, or you may not be in the correct directory. Check this by
escaping to the shell and trying some commands there, such as **!pwd**
or **!ls.**
   In general, if **ex** is given the name of a file that does not
exist, it assumes that you wish to create that file. If you quit the
session without a write, that file will not be created.
   The **e** command is useful when changing files frequently. But
before moving to the next file, you must save the current file with
w, if it has been altered. If you do not save the file, **ex** will send
you a warning, as happens with **q.**

```
:e file-2                              = change file
"file-2" 4 lines, 23 characters
....................                   = alterations
:e file-3
No write since last change (:edit! overrides)
```

12.3.2 Command w (continued)
Command **w**, without argument, writes to the previously designated
file. If you supply a file name, the contents of the buffer memory
will be saved under this name. This is another way of making a copy
of a file.

```
:e like-this                           = file to be edited
"like-this" 4 lines, 23 characters
```

```
:w like-that                            = a copy is made
"like-that" [New file] 4 lines, 23 characters
```

You can tell **w** to save from one specified line to another. To transfer a fragment of text to a safety file, for example, from the current line to the end, we build the command as follows.

```
.,$w a.part                             = partial save
```

12.4 Moving to write mode: i

You have learnt command **a** for entering write mode. There is another command, **i**, which is similar; again, the period is used at the beginning of the line to return to the editing mode. The difference between the two lies in the fact that **i** allows writing before the current line, whereas command **a** adds after the current line.

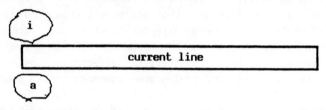

If you are writing to a new file, you can begin with **i** or with **a**. If you want to insert something in front of line 1, the best procedure is

```
li                                      = insert before line 1
Here is new line 1
.                                       = period to exit
```

12.5 Replacing lines: c

A line or a sequence of lines can be replaced by the command **c**. A period is required at the beginning of the line in order to exit, as with **a** and **i**. The simplest example is changing the current line.

```
c
I replace the current line
by these lines
.                                       = period to exit
```

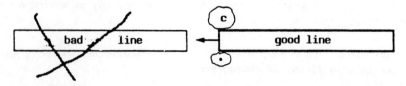

Lines 2 to 5 will be replaced by everything that precedes the single period at the beginning of the line.

```
2,5c
tralala
.
```

You can replace lines by means of **d** and **a** (or **i**), but **c** is more direct. In addition, for a partial change to a line, this command is sometimes better than a painstaking substitution with **s**. If a line contains special symbols, do not hesitate to make use of this command instead of straining to substitute them using a backslash.

12.6 Special characters in write mode
In write mode, all metacharacters regain their original meaning (with no interpretation), with exception of

- the character correction symbol
- the line correction symbol
- the backslash

What does one do though when one wants to use the hash in its literal sense (that is, as the delete symbol)? The answer is to precede it with a backslash.

```
a
(1) = \#
.
p                                        = verify
(1) = #
```

12.7 Inserting a file: r
Inserting an existing file into work that is currently being edited can save effort. The command **r** (read) is used for this task.

```
:! pwd > whereamI                 = create a file
:r whereamI                       = put it here
"whereamI" 1 line, 13 characters  = characters and lines read
:p
/users/moira                      = here are the contents read
```

In this example, we have created a small file outside the editor, using escape. Then the command **r** has read it in its totality and has added it to the end of the current file. The command displays the size of the file read as a total number of lines and characters.

After the read operation, the line pointer of the current file is
located at the last line read; this is displayed by **p.**

For **r** to function properly in the **ed** editor, the file must first
exist, and its name must be given without using metacharacters, because **r** does not do file name expansions.

```
r whe*                             = not known
/
```

In **ex,** this will function correctly.

When specifying the line number in front of **r,** you can choose
where to insert the file. The file will be placed after the
designated line.

```
Or whereamI                        = zero followed by r
19                                 = characters read
```

If you want to add this small file to the place where you are,
you will key.

```
.r whereamI                             = insert file here
```

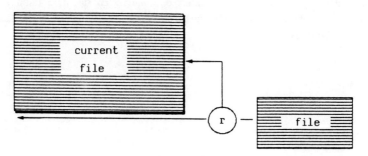

12.8 Moving lines: m

You can move one or more lines using the command **m.** This command
requires two addresses, the one in front of it being the source, the
other after it being the destination. Any address absent will be
taken to be the current line and the pointer will appear on the last
line to be moved. Here are some simple examples.

```
1m$                                = move line 1 to end
3m.                                = move line 3 after current line
```

To move several lines at once, we use a comma in the address notation to separate the beginning and the end of the section to be transferred.

3,6m9   = move lines 3 to 6 after 9

Can you decipher the operation obtained with the following instructions?

.,.+5m$-1

Solution: This instruction will move the lines starting at the current line and ending 5 lines on, placing them after the penultimate line.

Here are two more lines to interpret.

m.+1   = m+
m.-2   = m--

Solution: The first swaps the current line with the one that immediately precedes it; the second does the same but with the next line.

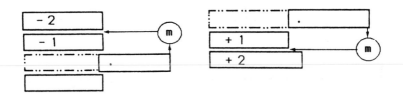

12.9 Transferring lines: t

The command **t** (transfer) has the effect of duplicating one or more lines. The syntax is identical to **m**, but this command leaves the original line(s) unaltered.

t.   = make a copy
.,/I am/t$

The first command copies the current line after the current line. This a way of duplicating it. The second command copies the set of lines, from the current line to the one containing 'I am' to the end of the text.

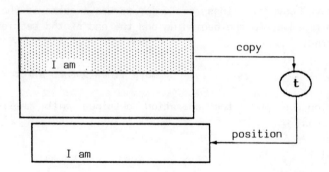

12.10 Joining lines: j

Command **j** (join) allows you to merge contiguous lines into one.

  If you want to obtain a single line from a block of lines, you must specify the address (beginning and end, separated by a comma). There is no need to insert **p** immediately after **j**, as it will automatically display the result.

```
:e standing                        = new file
"standing" No such file or directory
:a                                 = write mode
L                                  = first line
Y
I
N
G
.                                  = last line
:1,$j                              = merge all
L Y I N G                          = the result
```

  Note that **j** will only join lines that follow one another.

```
:7,8p                              = display
we are not
separated
:-                                 = move back one line
we are not
:j                                 = join
we are not separated               = inserts space between joined lines
```

12.11 See invisible characters: l

It is difficult to identify visually spaces from tabulations, but the computer has no difficulty, because each has a different ASCII code. The command l (list) will display non-printable characters using visible symbols.

If your terminal behaves as UNIX intends, a tabulation will represented with >, while a space and other non-printable characters will be displayed in octal code preceded by a backslash.

If a substitution command s does not succeed, check the line with the l command in order to find any non-printable character. If there are any, make the substitution using that 'Jack of all characters', the period, in the place where the problem lies.

12.12 Cancel the previous operation: u

However attentive you are, errors will occur when editing text. There is a very useful command u (undo) which allows you to cancel the the substitution you have just made. u will show the last line of the reinstated result. It can also operate with other commands, for example, **a,c,d,j,m,r,s,t,** etc.

12.13 File name: f

After frequent changes of file, using **e** for example, you may well find that you have forgotten the name of the current file. The command **f** will provide this for you.

```
:f                                      = ??
test                                    = 'test' is the file
```

If you designate a name after **f,** this name will given to the current file.

```
:f forget-me-not                        = change of name
```


12.14 Summary

We have examined line addressing within **ex.** Most of the commands require the address to be placed immediately in front of them. These are the symbols to be remembered.

```
$       last line
+       forward
-       back
/ab/    context 'ab'
=       display line number
```

We have introduced some additional commands:

c   replace lines
f   display or change name of current file
i   insert lines
j   join lines
l   display non-printable characters
m   move lines
r   insert a file
t   duplicate lines
u   undo previous operation

13 More on editing

13.0 Session aim

We shall use regular expressions (introduced in session 11) to locate lines by context.

We shall also deal with the problem of special characters that can be difficult to use with the substitution **s** or global **g** commands.

We shall introduce another editor, **sed.**

13.1 Referring to a line

You know how to search for a string of characters in the text by using slashes: /string/. The line pointer will move to the next line containing that string.

```
:e astrology                            = create file
"astrology" No such file or directory   = yes, it's new
:a                                      = write mode
First decan:                            = start of text
an emotional problem ought to be solved.
Second decan:
a favourable sun strengthens your authority.
Third decan:
Saturn is guarding your rear.
.                                       = end of text
:w                                      = save file
"astrology" [New file] 6 lines, 156 characters
```

Now that the file is written, we can do a context search. We can place a **regular expression** made up of metacharacters between slashes, but for the moment we will use normal characters.

```
:/decan:/                               = search instruction
First decan:                            = there you are
```

After being read by **w**, the pointer is located at the end of the file. The search command has sent it back to the beginning; we made a loop.

13.1.1 Sequence //

In this same example, in order to go to the second 'decan', we do not have to key in the string a second time.

```
://                                    = /decan:/
Second decan:
```

Here **ex** has memorised the expression and the repeated slash has indicated to it that we are seeking the same string, further on.

```
://
Third decan:
://
First decan:                          = the loop is closed
```

13.1.2 Sequence ??

You can even invert the direction of the search by using the repeated question mark.

```
:??                                    = let's go back
Third decan:
:??
Second decan:
```

13.2 Replacing a string: s (continued)

The memorised expression can also be used in the substitution command.

```
://                                    = search
Third decan:
:s//Decan:/p                           = replacement
Third Decan:
```

The memorisea expression has been replace by the string 'Decan'. For the next occurrence of the string, we can provide a more compact instruction.

```
://s//Decan:/p                         = decan: -> Decan:
First Decan:
```

This command line is read as follows: the system looks for the line containing the memorised expression (first pair of slashes); if the line is found, **s** requests the expression (second pair of slashes) to be replaced by the specified string, then displayed (**p**).

If we had keyed the instruction '//s///', the pointer would have
gone to the line where 'decan:' was found (// before **s**) and would
have replaced this (// after **s**) with nothing (/ at the end); 'decan'
would therefore have disappeared.

```
//s///
```

13.2.1 Cutting a line in two

There is no command that carries out the opposite of the **j** command.
It is somewhat difficult to obtain the same effect. The method is to
insert a Return in the middle of the line. We shall put the following two words on two lines, using **ed**

```
p
one part
s/one /one                               = CR
?
```

If you press Return in the right-hand string, **ed** sends ?, because
the command line has been taken to be non-terminated. **ex**, on the
other hand, assumes that you have missed out the terminator and
pretends that there was one. Remember that for the insertion command
we have learnt to use a backslash in front of a special character.
You can now proceed in a similar manner.

```
:p
one part
:s/one pa/ one \
pa/p
part
:.-1,.p
one
part
```

13.2.2 Special characters

Special symbols can be used to facilitate line searching. We shall
re-examine some of the **grep** metacharacters (cf session 11.6), before
introducing new ones.

  ^ start of line symbol
  $ end of line symbol
  . any character
  * repeat preceding character

Notes
(1) /^$/ indicates an empty line.
(2) If a sequence of characters occurs more than once in a line, avoid any confusion by combining your command with **$** to indicate the end of line.

:p
To be, or not to be
:s/be$/, that is the question/p
To be, or not to , that is the question

(3) Some further explanation of **$**, which has different meanings according to the context. Take this example

:$s/$/$/
To be, or not to , that is the question$

   As address element (first **$**), the dollar represents the last line of text in the buffer memory. On the other hand at the line level, this sign represents the end of the edited line (second **$**). The dollar keeps its literal sense in write mode (under **a,c,** and l), or in the right-hand string in in the substitution (last **$**). All this complication only adds the **$** sign at the end of the last line.

(4) A period followed by an asterisk signifies any string.

:p
I am fat, but you are like a pole
:s/fat.*re //p   = this part is deleted
I am like a pole   = diet succeeds

Symbol **&**
To change the form 'changed' into 'unchanged', the traditional instruction is

:s/changed/unchanged/p
unchanged

   But **ex** offers you another possibility using **&**, the symbol that represents the left-hand string.

:s/changed/un&/p
unchanged

   On the other hand, if you want to use the symbol in its original sense, you have to remove its special meaning by placing a backslash in front of it. Otherwise, you will get results like this.

```
:s/Laurel and Hardy/Laurel & Hardy/p
Laurel Laurel and Hardy Hardy
```

   Apart from this symbol & and the backslash, the metacharacters have no special meaning when part of the right-hand string. They only play a part in the right-hand string. To make things easier to follow, we can say that the left-hand string is the edit string and the right-hand string is the write string. You will recall that the metacharacters function with the commands in edit mode and that in write mode all the symbols are general purpose. The correction characters and the backslash operate in both modes.

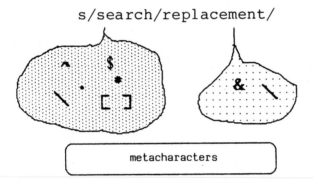

metacharacters

Backslash
If a line contains a slash, it can be cancelled by a backslash. In order to change the following division into multiplication, '2/3' into '2*3', the command will need to be

```
:s/2\/3/2*3/p
2*3
```

   A simpler method is to use a different character as the separator, such as :, i, %, etc, as long as it does not appear in the edit string or the write string.

```
:s:2/3:2*3:p                              = more intelligible
2*3
```

For an inverse operation (for example, * to \), we need to neutralise the asterisk which is a metacharacter in the left-hand string

```
:s:2\*:x/:p
x/3
```

If you are fearful of getting into a mess when replacing a string in a line, destroy the line with **d** and rewrite it with **a** or **i**, or, simpler still, replace it with **c**.

13.3 Global replacement: g

When you want to change a sequence of characters in a section of the file, you must begin the command line with the address that ind-icates the start and end of the section to which the command will relate.

```
:1,$p
opus 54 opus   67
opus 89 opus 121
:1,$s/opus/OPUS/p                    = substitution
OPUS 89 opus 121
:1,$p                                = verification
OPUS 54 opus   67
OPUS 89 opus 121
```

This is perhaps not the effect expected. The replacement has only been made on the first occurrence. To obtain repeated substitution on the same line, we should use the **g** (global) suffix.

```
:1,$s/opus/OPUS/gp
OPUS 89 OPUS 121
:1,$p
OPUS 54 OPUS   67
OPUS 89 OPUS 121
```

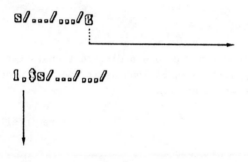

An operation repeated on a certain number of lines can be made
with the prefix **g** command, placed in front of a string, followed by
one or more commands. We will search globally for the lines that
contain the regular expresion 'Dec*'.

```
:g/Dec.*/p
First Decan:
Second Decan:
Third Decan:
```

   You will now appreciate the naming of the **grep** command that we
touched upon in session 11.
   Instead of **p,** we can write **s,** for example. Let us move back to
lower case.

```
:1,$p                                   = text as it now stands
OPUS 54 OPUS   67
OPUS 89 OPUS 121
:g/OPUS/s//opus/p                       = substitution
opus 54 OPUS   67
opus 89 OPUS 121
```

   As the above display shows, the **g** prefix only operates on the
first occurrence of the specified string in the line. To ensure that
all occurrences in the line are changed, **g** must also be taken as a
suffix.

```
:g/OPUS/s//opus/gp
opus 54 opus   67
opus 89 opus 121
```

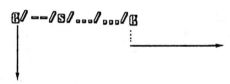

   The difference between '1,$' and the g prefix relates to the dis-
play of the results produced. With '1,$...p', only the last line to
be affected will be displayed; on the other hand, **g** displays all
lines involved.
   Here are some other examples of **g** with the command **d.** The
following instructions will delete those lines that only contain
'.sp 1'.

```
:g/^.sp 1$/d
```

Note that the undo command **u** only functions for the very last operation carried out by **g**. To return to the initial position, it would be better to go out of **ed** without saving and then return.

13.4 Stream editing: sed

sed is a non-interactive text editor that is intended chiefly for correcting existing text. Its use is based on **ed**, and you first need to master **ed** (or **ex**) thoroughly, before embarking upon it.

Its main feature is to through the text line by line, hence the name Stream EDitor.

sed instructions, which are analogous to those of **ed** (and **ex**), are transmitted either on the command line that calls the editor, or in a separate file that is sent to **sed.**

It is sensible to use **sed** in the following cases.

(1) For large files. Thanks to the stream handling, there is no limit to the size of the file, in contrast to the situation with **ed/ex.**

(2) For editing instructions that are too complicated, They can be put into a file (a facility also available under **ed/ex**).

(3) For handling several files in a single pass. The files can simply be listed in a command line.

(4) Included in a pipeline, **sed** is a powerful tool for handling strings of characters. It can be used as a filter to edit or to alter part of a file during the execution of pipeline processes.

We will illustrate this with a simple example. The results will be displayed at the standard output.

```
$ echo aaa > a-nothing                = we create a file
$ sed -e s/a/HA/g a-nothing           = change
HAHAHA                                 = a joke
$cat a-nothing
aaa                                    = original file unchanged
$
```

The option **-e** indicates that what follows is a **sed** instruction. When there is only one instruction on the command line, this option can be omitted: sed s/a/HA/ **a-nothing** would have been enough.

```
$ echo bbb >> a-nothing                   = addition to the file
$ sed -e s/a/A/ -e s/b/B/g a-nothing > waste-bin
```

```
$ cat waste-bin
Aaa
BBB
$
```

If the **sed** instruction contains special instructions like space (blank or tabulation), it must be placed within single or double quotes.

```
$ sed -e "s/a/a /g" a-nothing
a a a
bbb
$
```

UNIX special characters must be preceded with a backslash as in **ed** or **ex**.
We now examine use of a file containing correction instructions for **sed**.

```
$ cat > change
s/a/a*/g
s:b:b/:g
$                                = CTRL-D
```

To mention this instructions file, we insert the **-f** option, followed by the name of the instructions file.

```
$ sed -f change a-nothing
a*a*a*
b/b/b/
$
```

The **sed** editor copies all the input lines to the standard output, even if we only specify a part of the file to be displayed.

```
$ sed lp a-nothing
aaa
aaa
bbb
$
```

The **q** (quit) command allows you to exit from **sed** after the system has displayed the number of lines specified by the figure in front of **q**.

```
$ cat > forall
11
22
33
$                                        = CTRL-D
$ sed 2q forall
11
22
$
```

On the other hand, if you want to display lines 2 and 3, the '2,3p' method is not suitable.

```
$ sed 2,3p forall
11
22
22
33
33
$
```

You therefore have to override the 'normal' output (display of all lines) and use the option **-n** to cause only the specified lines to be displayed.

```
$ sed -n 2,3p forall
22
33
$
```

Here is an example using a pipeline. We have mentioned above (cf session 3.5) that the most important commands are held in the /bin directory. We will look at the first ten. This is how the system should respond, more or less (a simulation of the command **head** under UCB UNIX).

```
$ ls /bin | sed 10q
[
adb
ar
as
awk
cat
cc
chgrp
```

chmod
cmp
$

13.5 Summary

We have deepened our knowledge of addressing and referencing lines.

We have returned to the substitution command **s** to learn how the metacharacters behave.

We have studied the following commands:

l display invisible characters
u cancel previous operation
g global operation.

We have also examined **sed**, the stream editor.
We have tried out these commands:

s substitution
p display
q quit

We have studied these options:

-e instruction on command line
-f instruction in a file
-n override of normal output.

Symbols used in ed/ex

	Meaning	Examples
/	normal string delimiter	
	(other symbols possible)	:;.etc
,	address separator	1,3p
.	current line	.,$p 1,.d
=	display line number	.= $= /str/=
Δ	beginning of line	/Δ4/d
$	end of line	s/end,$/end, /
#	last line	1,$p
−	backwards	.-9,.p
+	forwards	.,+9p
//	searches downstream from	
	specified string;	
	empty string	s/str//p
??	searches upstream from	
	specified string	
&	repeat left-hand string	s/mat/&ch/p
\	neutralise a metacharacter	s/*/asterisk/p

List of commands under ed/ex

X:	begin address
Y:	end address
Z:	target address
:	string of characters
():	optional elements
fi:	file name

	Meaning	Examples		
a	addition after current line	a text .	Xa text .	
c	replacement of lines	c text .	Xc text .	X,Yc text .
d	destruction of lines	d(p)	Xd(p)	X,Yd(p)
e	editing a file	e fi		
f	display file name	f		
	change file name	f fi		
g	global operation	g/st/p	g/st/d	g/st/s/ stl/st2/g(p)
i	insertion before current line	i text .	Xi text .	
j	join lines	j(p)	Xj(p)	X,Yj(p)
l	display invisible characters	l	Xl	X,Yl
m	move lines	mZ	XmZ	X,YmZ
p	display lines	p	Xp	X,Yp
q	exit from editor	q		
r	insert a file	rfi	Xrfi	
s	replace characters	s/stl/st2/(p)		
t	duplicate lines	tZ	XtZ	X,Ytz
u	undo preceding operation	u(p)		
w	save file	w(fi)	X,Yw(fi)	

14 Properly your own

14.0 Session aim
We return to the **nroff** text formatter; first, page formatting with the help of **ms** macros; then, basic **nroff** instructions.

14.1 ms macros
Text presentation is achieved by means of standard pre-programmed macro instructions (henceforth called macros) that are accessible from the **–ms** option of **nroff.** These macros are found in the file called **tmac.s** of the directory **/usr/lib/tmac.**

14.1.1 Initialisation
To obtain the best results from **ms**, it is preferable to set up the page formatting parameters in front of the first line of text. Use one of the following macros: **.LP, .PP, .NH** (see later), or **.TL**, which can take other functions but restore these parameters to their default values.

14.1.2 Paragraph control
There are several instructions for formatting a paragraph: **.PP, .LP, .IP**, etc. You just need to place one of them before the first line of the paragraph. These instructions routinely insert a space in front of the first line of the paragraph.

Paragraph with first line indented:
First, the instruction **.PP** (ParagraPh) causes the first line of a paragraph to be indented from the left margin. This instruction must be placed on its own line, at the beginning, and preceding the para-graph.

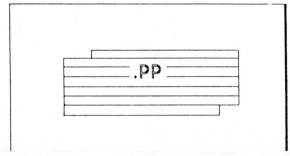

Paragraph ranged to left margin:
If you want the first line of a paragraph to align with the left
margin (blocked), you should use **.LP** (Left-aligned Paragraph).

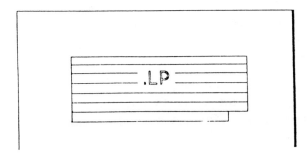

Indented paragraph:
The instruction **.IP** causes all the lines in a paragraph to be indented.

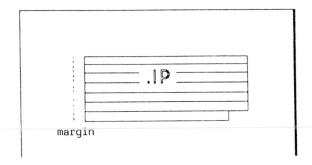

margin

If you place a string after **.IP**, the first line will not be indented, which is a useful way of creating the effect of enumeration.

```
.nr LL 40n                    = line length 40 characters
.IP (1)
INTERFACE:
A boundary between two devices or two pieces of software
across which the form and functions of the
signals that pass it are specified.
.IP (2)
MODEM:
A piece of equipment that converts digital signals
into analogue signals for transmission.
```

This will give:

(1)   INTERFACE: A boundary between two
       devices or two pieces of software
       across which the form and functions
       of the signals that pass it are
       specified.

(2)   MODEM: A piece of equipment that
       converts   digital   signals   into
       analogue signals for transmission.

Nested indented paragraph:
In order to obtain an indented paragraph within a paragraph that is
itself already indented, you need to use two instructions:

.RS (Right Shift) start right shift
.RE (Right shift End) end right shift

Here is an example

```
.LP
Data subjects
.IP (I)
Should know
.RS
.IP -
what information about them is held
.IP -
why it is held
.IP -
who will use it
.RE
.IP (II)
Should be able to check that
.RS
.IP -
the information is correct
.IP -
only relevant data are used for a defined purpose
.RE
```

Result:

Data subjects

(I)   Should know

-   what information about them is held

-   why it is held

-   who will use it

(II) Should be able to check that

-   the information is correct

-   only relevant data are used for a defined purpose

Numbering paragraphs:
The instruction **.NH** (Numbered Heading) sees to the automatic numbering of paragraphs to five levels of complexity. For example, the
following sequence

.NH
Tango
.NH 2
History
.NH 2
Rhythm
.NH 2
Variations
.NH 3
Argentine step
.NH 3
Habanera

will produce the following output

1.   Tango
1.1.   History
1.2.   Rhythm
1.3.   Variations
1.3.1.   Argentine step
1.3.2.   Habanera

Displayed paragraph:
Quoted text should often be displayed with indentation to the left
and to the right. To achieve this, the instructions **.QS** and **QE** must
be placed respectively before and after the paragraph to be
displayed.

.LP
What is the most important factor in a software project?
To quote B.W. Boehm:
.QS
Without doubt the quality of the personnel has the most important
influence on a project.
(Proceedings of TRW Symposium, 1974)
.QE
We may ask if this is still true.

What is the most important factor in a software project?

    To quote B.W. Boehm: Without doubt the quality of the
    personnel has the most important influence on a project.
    (Proceedings of TRW Symposium, 1974)

We may ask if this is still true.

Retaining whole paragraphs:
In order to avoid a paragraph being broken between one page and the
next, two instructions can be used. These are **.KS** (Keep Start)   and
.KE (Keep End).

.KS
artificial intelligence
is the opposite of natural stupidity
(quoted by J.C. Rault, "Systemes experts : perspectives
industrielles", 1985)
.KE

    Depending on the space available, the text will be printed on the
current page or taken on to the next page.

Illustration paragraphs:
Examples often need to be presented in an indented paragraph, but
without right-hand justification. In this case the instructions **.DS**
(Display Start) and **.DE** (Display End) are used.

```
.LP
Example:
.DS
12+21 = 33
123 + 321 = 444
1234 + 4321 = 5555
12345 + 54321 = 66666
.DE
Commentary:
```

This gives

Example:

```
        12+21 = 33
        123 + 321 = 444
        1234 + 4321 = 5555
        12345 + 54321 = 66666
```

Commentary:

14.1.3 Changing registers

For those users who are even more perfectionist, it should be noted
that some macro registers can be altered. These are

LL line length
PO left margin
HM top (Header) margin
FM margin at foot
PI size of indentation
FL length of footnote

In order to alter these numerical macro registers, you insert the
desired value plus, without space, i (for the number of inches) or,
n (for the number of characters).

```
.nr FL 7i                  = footnote length 7 inches
.nr FL 60n                 = footnote length 60 characters
.nr PI 0.5i                = indent half an inch
```

It is preferable to initialise parameters in ordinary **nroff**
instructions, if possible; for example, with **.ll** or **.po,** instead of
LL and **PO.** This is because there is some delay before macros take
effect (this will be examined more closely later).

14.1.4 Various instructions

In addition to the **.ND** (No Date) instruction, there is the **.DA** instruction which prints the date in the form that you prefer. It must be inserted at the beginning of the input text.

.DA 14 7 1986

Resulting from the fact that **ms** was perfected for the publication of articles by Bell Laboratories staff, there are several useful instructions for the preparation of scientific documents.

.TL title centred
.AU author's name centred
.AI organisation's name centred

These three instructions must appear before the line to which they refer.

14.2 Basic nroff instructions (continued)

For detailed control of your text layout, you need to make use of the basic **nroff** instructions.

14.2.1 Page control

Page presentation:
The following are the main instructions for page formatting (some have been mentioned already in session 5).

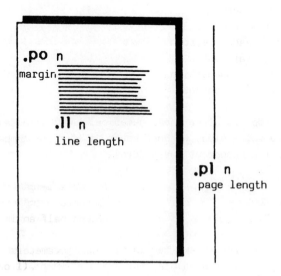

.pl n   page length, n lines
.po n   page offset (left margin), n characters
.ll n   line length, n characters

The current value of **.pl** is from 66 to 72; this is the maximum number of lines per page. If you change it rashly, you may find that the system's pages do not coincide with the paper printout.

Depending on the context, those instructions that take a numerical argument, such as **.po** and **.ll** can be altered in absolute or relative value, using the + or - sign with reference to their initial value.

.ll 66

. . . .

.ll -10   = line shortened by 10 characters (56)

. . . .

.ll +10   = return to original value (66)

Vertical spacing:
Inter-linear spacing is controlled by **.ls** (line space).

.ls 2   = 1 interline
.ls 3   = 2 interlines

Page change:
The instruction **.bp** causes the formatter to begin a new page.

In order to avoid a new paragraph starting on the last line of a page, nroff can be instructed to reserve a minumum of say 5 lines for a paragraph. **.ne** (need) sees to this; if there is insufficient room, **nroff** goes to a new page.

.ne 5   = print on this page if 5 lines remain;
                                 otherwise, take new page

Pagination:
You can print one line, divided into three parts, in the top margin of each page. The instruction **.tl** (title line) takes care of this. The three parts must be separated by an apostrophe; they will be justified, respectively, to the left, to the centre and to the right. Two successive apostrophes indicate an empty field. The page number, which is symbolised by %, can be placed in one of these fields; it will automatically be replaced with the correct page number when the processing begins.

.tl 'X'Y'Z'X'

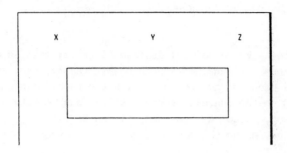

```
.tl ''Page%''                        = page number in middle
.tl 'Chapter 2''- % -'               = page number on right
```

The page numbering starts at 1 by default. If you want to alter this, you use the **.nr** (numeric register) instruction followed by the name of the register and the figure of your choice.

```
.nr % 55                             = page numbering starts at 55
```

14.2.2 Justification
Justification consists in inserting appropriate spaces between words on the line, so that left and right hand margins are aligned and the text is pleasingly and readably presented. These are the instructions.

```
.na     no adjustment (no justification)
.ad     adjust (justify)
.ce n   centre n lines
```

Under **nroff** **.ad** is implicit. When **.na** is invoked, the right-hand margin remains ragged.
    .ce defaults to one line if no number is specified.

14.2.3 Indentation
Indentation is a shifting in relation to the left-hand margin. The instruction **.in** inserts the number of spaces specified in the argument throughout the remaining text, or until a new **.in** is encountered. The argument can be an absolute or a relative value (number of characters).

```
.in 8                   = indent 8 characters from left margin
.in -3                  = reduce indent by 3 characters
```

If you only want to indent one line, you should use the **.ti** (temporary indent) instruction. The line that follows **.ti** will be indented by the number of characters that you specify.

```
.ll 40
.in 5
.ti -5
GATEWAY:
A computer system or exchange
in one network that allows access
to and from another network.
```

will produce:

```
GATEWAY: A computer system  or  exchange
        that  allows  access  to  and  from
        another network.
```

14.2.4 Line control
To control the filling of output lines, there are the following instructions

.fi fill line completely
.nf no fill
.br break and go to new line

Filling:
Normally, with **.fi** operative, the **nroff** processor fills the line to the full. The effect of **.nf** is to cancel this instruction and it allows the output of the line to appear just as it is held in the file.

For example, if you want to obtain a pseudo underlining effect with any character,

```
LIKE THIS
*********
```

If you forget to insert **.nf**, you will get

```
LIKE THIS*********
```

Return to line:
.br returns you to the beginning of the next line.

Also, if the first character is a space, the line will also start with a space. One or two lines will appear as in the input text.

Underlining:
The instruction **.ul**, followed by a numeric argument, underlines the number of lines specified.

```
.fi
do
.ul 1
not
underline
```

will give

do <u>not</u> underline

Skip a line:
.sp   skips a line
.sp n   skips n lines.

14.2.5 Breaking a word at the end of a line
In order to fill a line, **nroff** breaks a word that will not fit, under the control of the instruction **.nh**. This may or may not be desirable, in which case you have the option of the **.nh** instruction.

.nh no hyphenation
.hy hyphenation yes.

14.3 Summary
We have studied the following **nroff** instructions in this session.

ms macros:
.PP   paragragh with first line indented
.LP   paragraph ranged left
.IP (str) paragraph indented (string)
.RS   indented paragraph right shifted, start
.RE   indented paragraph right shifted, end
.NH n   numbered paragraph (n = 1 to 5)
.QS   quoted paragraph, start
.QE   quoted paragraph, end
.DS   display paragraph, start
.DE   display paragraph, end
.FS   footnote, start

.FE	footnote, end
.KS	keep paragraph, start
.KE	keep paragraph, end
.DA	date
.ND	no date
.TL	title centred
.AU	author centred
.AI	organisation centred

The numeric registers that can be altered:

LL	line length
PO	page offset (left margin)
HM	header margin
FM	footer margin
PI	paragraph indentation
FL	footnote length

The basic **nroff** instructions:

.pl n	page length, n lines
.po n	page offset (left margin), n characters
.ll n	line length, n characters
.bp	begin (new) page
.ne n	minimum n lines to print at foot of page
.na	no adjust (no justification)
.ad	return to justification
.ce n	centre n lines
.hy	hyphenate at line end
.nh	no hyphenation
.fi	fill line
.nf	no filling
.br	break to next line
.sp n	skip n lines
.ls n	n-1 interlines
.in (+-)	indent n charcters
.ti n	indent n characters on next line
.tl'a'b'c'	define top line under three headings
.nr r n	load n into register r
.so file	insert a file (cf 15.2)

15 Completing the picture

15.0 Session aim
We shall suggest some ideas for the more efficient use of **nroff**: organising files and options.

The last part of the session will be devoted to the formatting of tables with the processor **tbl**.

15.1 Initialisation file
There are certain instructions that are only used at the start of a section of text, but whose effects relate to the text in its entirety; for example, line length, page length, inter-linear spacing, etc. Such instructions are best placed in a small separate file.

```
.LP                                = implicit initialisation
.nh                                = no hyphenation
.ND                                = no date
......
.....
```

15.2 Everything in a file
When lengthy text is involved, it is sensible and practical to divide it into several parts that are held in different files. This is because dealing with a small amount of text at a time has its advantages: operations with the editor are more convenient, the risk of any accident is minimised and the **nroff** processing of the material is faster, etc. However, in order to output all the files, the **nroff** command line inevitably becomes more complicated:

```
nroff -ms my.init intro chap1 chap2 ... | lpr
```

nroff offers an alternative. The instruction **.so** allows the file to be read as a data source. It creates a file which calls all the necessary files for the processing. For example

```
$ cat alltext
.so my.init                        = initialisation file
.so intro                          = first text file
.so chap1
.so chap2
.so chap3
....
.so conclusion
$
```

The instruction to proceed could not be simpler

```
$ nroff -ms alltext
```

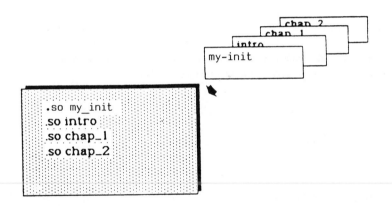

15.3 nroff options: -o -n

Here are some options for **nroff** that control the output.

The system can be instructed to produce only those pages that you require. The **-o** (output) option sees to this; it is followed by the page number. This saves time and paper, especially if the alterations are localised.

```
$ nroff -o5 chap1                  = produce page 5
$ nroff -o5,8 chap1                = pages 5 and 8
$ nroff -o5-7 chap1                = pages 5,6 and 7
$ nroff -o-5 chap1                 = from start to page 5
$ nroff -o18- chap1                = from page 18 to end
```

If you adopt implicit paging, you can specify the page number of the first output page using option **-n**; for example, '-n14'. This is convenient when you are extracting a long piece of text from several different files, but with continuous paging.

15.4 Producing tables: tbl

Producing a table with a text editor is tedious, even with the help of tabulation. UNIX offers the special program **tbl**, for this task.

Generally, text and tables are held together in a file. With tables, you need to insert some instructions immediately in front of the data, to specify its layout.

```
text
.TS                                         = start table
options;
format.
data...
data...
.TE                                         = end table
text continues
```

Here is an example of what actual instructions might look like (without preceding and following text).

```
.TS
box tab(:);
clr.
Program:Author:Year
.sp 1
nroff:M.E.Lesk:1974
tbl:M.E.Lesk:1979
eqn.B.W.Kernighan:1975
.TE
```

As we are here dealing with a **nroff** preprocessor, you first have to connect **tbl** and **nroff**, then add first another filter called **col** (cf 15.5).

```
$ tbl table | nroff | col
```

Program	Author	Year
nroff	M.E.Lesk	1974
tbl	M.E.Lesk	1979
eqn	B.W.Kernighan	1975

15.4.1 Start and end of table

If we look at the table file again, we see that the instructions **.TS** and **.TE** are provided to indicate to **tbl** the beginning and end of the table. Here again, any spaces in front of these instructions will prevent the normal operation of **tbl.** If you do not position these two instructions correctly, you will be sadly disappointed by your output.

15.4.2 Options

The options relate to the specifications that apply to the complete table, that is, the appearance of the table, the nature of its border and its position on the page.

We have chosen **box** in our example; this draws two horizontal and two vertical lines that frame the data. Our second option is the field separator; after the keyword **tab,** the colon (as selected here) is placed within brackets. The **tab** instruction is unnecessary if you are using normal tabulation (TAB or CTRL-1) to key the data.

The options line must terminate with a semi-colon.

15.4.3 Format

The format line specifies the position of the data on the line for each field. These are the possible arguments:

c   centre
l   range left
r   range right
n   numeric alignment

The format line must terminate with a period.

A vertical bar can be placed between these arguments in order to obtain a vertical rule between two columns. Thus, for the following

```
$ $ cat table
.TS
box tab(:);
c|l|r.
Program:Author:Year
.sp 1
nroff:M.E.Lesk:1974
tbl:M.E.Lesk:1979
eqn:B.W.Kernighan:1975
.TE
```

the output will appear as follows

$ tbl table | nroff | col

Program	Author	Year
nroff	M.E.Lesk	1974
tbl	M.E.Lesk	1979
eqn	B.W.Kernighan	1975

15.5 Interference between tbl and nroff

If you try to begin the processing without **col,** you will be in for some surprises; the vertical bars will appear after the table in some place where they have nothing to do with the table. This is because the data and the frame are not treated as a whole; after printing the text, **nroff** goes back to print the box as specified by **box.** Since on many basic terminals this would not be possible, UNIX sets aside a **col** filter that overcomes this problem. The **col** command carries out what is equivalent to a backwards movement in the buffer memory. If the option **box** is omitted, it is not necessary to invoke this filter.

15.6 Summary

We have reviewed the following **nroff** options:

-o selective output
-n pagination.

We have examined the table formatter **tbl,** which has the following form:

```
.TS
options;
format.
data
.TE
```

these options:

box   frame
tab(:) type of tabulation;
;   end of options line

and this format:

c   centring
l   range left
r   range right
n   numeric alignment
.   end of format line

   Processing text that includes tables with the **box** option must be
done as follows:

tbl...   nroff...   col

Part 4   Everything you always wanted to know about the shell

16   A little procedure

16.0 Session aim
We shall learn how to edit and execute a shell procedure.

During this and subsequent sessions, we shall create a number of small files - our procedures. The sensible approach is to create a directory (with **mkdir**), then make it the current directory (with **cd**), before embarking on the essence of the subject. Here is the sequence

```
$ pwd                              = where are we?
/users/mike
$ mkdir test                       = creation of
$ cd test                          = directory
$                                  = ready
```

16.1 Definition
Up until now, we have seen the shell in an interactive context. We have entered each command at the keyboard and waited for the shell to read and execute it. In fact, the shell is much more than a simple interpreter of commands; it far exceeds the capabilities of many other operating systems.

The shell can read commands from a file. Let us create, using the text editor, a file called **mydate**, containing

```
date
```

We inform the shell that the commands are to be read from the **mydate** file, by keying

```
$ sh mydate                        = which should give
Wed Aug 27 10:13:31 BST 1986
$
```

The shell (command **sh**) has read **mydate** and has executed the only command it found there, **date**. The **mydate** file is called a shell procedure, or a command file, or a command procedure.

16.2 Executable status

A more convenient way of informing the shell that commands are to be read from a file is to make this file executable. To do this, we have already met the utility called **chmod** (see session 8).

```
$ chmod +x mydate                    = mydate is made executable
$
```

   Now, we only need to key

```
$ mydate                             = which should give
Wed Aug 27 10:13:41 BST 1986
$
```

   Of course, this change of mode need only be done once.
   When you create shell procedures, you often get the following message

```
sh : concerto : cannot execute
$
```

   This is because you have omitted to make the procedure (**concerto**, in this case) executable.
   It is also important to note that the file **mydate** is in the current directory (the one that you are currently in). The command **mydate** will only function if you are in this directory. For example

```
$ cd ..                              = we move to the parent directory
$ mydate                             = gives
mydate: not found
$ cd test                            = return to your directory
$
```

   In the parent directory, the shell was unable to find **mydate**. We shall see below what we have to do to be able to execute our commands from any directory. For the moment, and in the following sessions, we have to remain in the same directory; otherwise, the procedures we create will not be found by the shell.
   Once we are further advanced, if the occasion arises, any changes of directory will be clearly stated.

16.3 Further development

We have just created a new command, albeit a small one. We can now add to it, still using the text editor, by inserting some lines, such as

echo "When icicles hang by the wall"

and at the end

echo "And Dick the shepherd blows his nail"
echo "And Tom bears logs into the hall"

   If we now list **mydate,** we get

echo "When icicles hang by the wall"
date
echo "And Dick the shepherd blows his nail"
echo "And Tom bears logs into the hall"

   Although it has been modified, **mydate** still retains its executable status. If we try

```
$ mydate                            = this should give
When icicles hang by the wall
Wed Aug 27 10:14:42 BST 1986
And Dick the shepherd blows his nail
And Tom bears logs into the hall
$
```

   If that does not happen, check what you have in **mydate;** also,
check that all quote marks are there.
   The commands present in **mydate** have been executed one after the
other.
   Of course, you can redirect the input/outputs of the commands
specified in the procedure. If we alter **mydate** to obtain

```
echo > winter
date >> winter
echo >> winter
echo >> winter
```

on the first line, the standard output of **echo** is directed to the
winter file; then the standard output of **date** is directed to the end
of **winter;** similarly, for the standard output of **echo** on the third
and fourth lines. If we now key

```
$ mydate                            = we get
$
```

Now check what is in **winter**

$ cat winter   = which should give

Wed Aug 27 10:15:23 BST 1986

$

    Furthermore, we can use a pipe. Let us make a file called **long**,
containing

echo "They sailed away for a year and a day" | wc -w

and make it executable with **chmod**; then initiate the command

$ chmod +x long
$ long   = gives
      9
$

that is, the number of words in the line.

16.4 One procedure may conceal another
The results so far may still not amount to much, but we should note
one thing already. Once it is made executable, a procedure is in-
distinguishable from a 'pure' program (that is, the result of the
compilation of a program written in Fortran, C, BASIC, etc). Thus,
you can very easily call a shell procedure from another procedure.
If we create a procedure called **doll1** and containing

echo "I am doll1"
doll2
echo "end of doll1"

and another procedure called **doll2**, containing

echo "I am doll2"
echo "end of doll2"

    After making them executable, we can now key

$ doll1   = which should give
I am doll1   = this is **doll1**
I am doll2   = this is **doll2**, executing

```
end of doll2                          = and stopping
end of doll1                          = return to doll1
$                                     = and end
```

There is almost no limit to the number of nestings.

In what follows, this similarity between a 'pure' program and a procedure will become greater, provided that we foster it. To anticipate a little, we shall sometimes use the term process interchangeably to describe a 'pure' program or a shell procedure.

16.5 Notes
The following points should be borne in mind throughout the next sessions.

(1) When executing the test procedures that follow, remain in the directory in which they were created (that is, the current directory).

(2) Do not give an existing name to a new procedure. For example, no **cat** or **ls** procedures.

16.6 Summary
You have learnt

a shell procedure (a sequence of commands to the shell)
the executable state (**chmod + x...**)

17 A procedure in search of input/output

17.0 Session aim
The purpose of this session is to master the standard input and output of a shell procedure, together with their effect on the standard input/outputs of the processes that make up a procedure.

17.1 Input/output of a shell procedure
In our previous attempts, we have scarcely considered inputs and outputs of shell procedures themselves. Now a procedure contains an input, a standard output and an error output, just like a 'pure' program (cf 2.1).

17.1.1 Standard output
We shall recreate the first procedure, namely the executable file **mydate** containing:

```
date
```

and try it, just like a 'pure' program:

```
$ mydate > bin                          = we get
$
```

UNIX has quietly handed control back to us. If we list the file **bin,** we find:

```
$ cat bin
Wed Aug 27 11:07:16 BST 1986            = gives us
$
```

Everything is as though the standard output of **date,** unassigned explicitly in our procedure, had also been edited on the **bin** file. This gives rise to this first rule (provisional at this stage, for the sake of simplicity):

In a procedure, the standard output of a process, which is explicitly unassigned, inherits the standard output of this procedure.

Inheritance of standard output

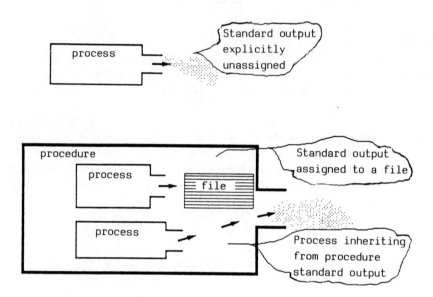

This is why until now our procedures were written to the screen. Because their standard output was not specified, it was therefore sent to the screen. Furthermore, because all the processes making up the procedure had their standard output 'free' (explicitly unassigned), they therefore inherited the standard output of the procedure, that is, the screen.

In what follows, we shall continue to use the term 'free' to describe a standard output (or an input) that is explicitly unassigned.

You will recall that only one of our procedures required redirections of the standard output of the processes that made it up.

```
echo "When icicles hang by the wall" > winter
date >> winter
echo "And Dick the shepherd blows his nail" >> winter
echo "And Tom bears logs into the hall" >> winter
```

This is the last version of **mydate** that wrote nothing on the screen. In fact, since the standard outputs were already assigned, they are not altered.

Let us try the following sequence:

```
$ mydate > verse
$ cat winter
When icicles hang by the wall
Wed Aug 27 11:08:03 BST 1986
And Dick the shepherd blows his nail
And Tom bears logs into the hall
$ cat verse
$
```

mydate has written nothing to its standard output, because none of the processes that go to make it up has its standard output 'free'.

Expressed in other words, internal redirections have priority.

It is worth explaining in greater detail what we understand by 'inherit the standard output of the procedure'. If we take the following version of **mydate**:

```
echo "When icicles hang by the wall"
date
echo "And Dick the shepherd blows his nail"
echo "And Tom bears logs into the hall"
```

in which three processes have their standard output 'free'. Now we key:

```
$ mydate > verse
$ cat verse                              = which gives
When icicles hang by the wall
Wed Aug 27 11:08:54 BST 1986
And Dick the shepherd blows his nail
And Tom bears logs into the hall
$
```

This might be what we expected; however, something strange has happened. The processes **echo** and **date** have written consecutively to **verse,** without overwriting the previous contents of **verse.** The result is therefore very different from this sequence:

```
$ echo "When icicles hang by the wall" > verse
$ date > verse
```

```
$ echo "And Dick the shepherd blows his nail" > verse
$ echo "And Tom bears logs into the hall" > verse
$
```

In this case, we would only have had the last line in **verse**.

Inheritance is in fact a much broader operation than pure and simple redirection; it embraces the reassignment of the output and of its context. Without going into too much detail, let us be reminded that this context includes a marker of the place in the output file (here **verse**) where the last write terminated. The next write will begin at that marker, and so on until the file is closed.

We will follow the marker step by step in our example (the backslash here represents a return to the line; the vertical arrow is our marker).

process	marker in verse	commentary
		= start of operations
		= **verse** (re)created
		= **verse** opened
		= marker Δ at start
echo "When.."		
	⇂ When..wall \	= First write
	⇂	
date		
	wall\Wed..1986 \	= Second write
	⇂	
echo "And.."		
	..1986\And..nail \	= Third write
	⇂	
echo "..hall"		
	..nail\And..hall \	= Fourth write
	⇂	= end of mydate
		= end of
		= verse

This shows why **verse** was full.

It is worth noting that the same thing occurs when commands are linked (session 9), as in

```
(pwd; ls) > file
```

Of course, it is only necessary to think about all of this if several processes have their output 'free' in a procedure. We shall see that this is quite rare in practice.

17.1.2 Standard input

The same applies to standard input. Let us create (and make executable) the following procedure, **counting**

```
wc -l > time                = counts lines read on its standard input
echo "lines have been counted" >> time
cat time
rm time                     = destroys time
```

and execute it

```
$ counting                  = nothing happens, no $
```

Why are we not handed back control? **wc** reads at its standard input, which is free, that **counting** has its standard input assigned to the keyboard; therefore **wc** goes to read the keyboard!

If, for example, we key

```
ab
c
zz                          = CTRL-D to terminate input
```

we shall read on the screen

```
     3
lines have been counted
$                           = control is handed back
```

We will now create a text file called **kingjohn,** which contains

```
Groom,
saddle
my faithful
charger.
```

and try it

```
$ counting < kingjohn              = should give
     4
lines have been counted
$
```

In fact, **wc** has inherited from the standard input of **counting,** redirected this time to the file **kingjohn.**

As with output, the inheritance of the input also includes its context, but here the consequences are more negative.

As before, the marker referred to above here points to that place in the file where the last read terminated.

Let us imagine the following procedure, called **recounting**, and containing

```
wc -l                                    = line count
wc -w                                    = word count
```

If we execute it on our **kingjohn** file

```
$ recounting < kingjohn
        4                                = we obtain no. of lines
        0                                = ?
$
```

Why do we get zero words? Let us work through the sequence

process	marker in kingjohn	commentary
		= start of
		= operations
	Groom..	= opening of
	⚡	= kingjohn
wc -l		= complete read
		= of kingjohn, Δ at end
	..charger. \	
	⚡	
wc -w		= nothing more to read

Since **wc -w** finds the end of a file, it returns a count of zero!

17.1.3 Error output

You will be right if you have guessed that everything that has been said about the standard output applies also for the error output.

Let us create the following procedure, called **tragedy**

```
cat king lear
```

which concatenates on the standard output the two files **king** and **lear.**
We then key

```
$ rm -f lear king                        = to ensure that
```

```
$ tragedy                              = they do not exist
cat: can't open king                   = gives
cat: can't open lear
$
```

These messages appear on the error output of **cat**, which has inherited from that of **tragedy**, namely the screen.

Redirection of the error output is shown by

```
2>
```

If we now try

```
$ tragedy 2> oblivion                  = redirect to oblivion
$ cat oblivion                         = gives
cat: can't open king
cat: can't open lear
$
```

17.1.4 Input and output

After these somewhat strange examples, let us return to some more
practical situations, using our initial **counting** procedure.

We shall now try the following combination, which is permissible
because **cat** has its output 'free'.

```
$ counting < kingjohn > bin
$
```

we list **bin**

```
$ cat bin
        4
lines have been counted
$
```

As expected, the standard output of **cat**, inheriting from that of
counting, has been directed to the file **bin**.

We can now update our rule on input/outputs:
Standard inputs and outputs, explicitly unassigned in a procedure,
inherit from the standard input and from the standard output of this
procedure.

This rule of inheritance remains valid at whatever level of
nesting one may find oneself when the procedure is called.

Example of multiple input/output inheritance

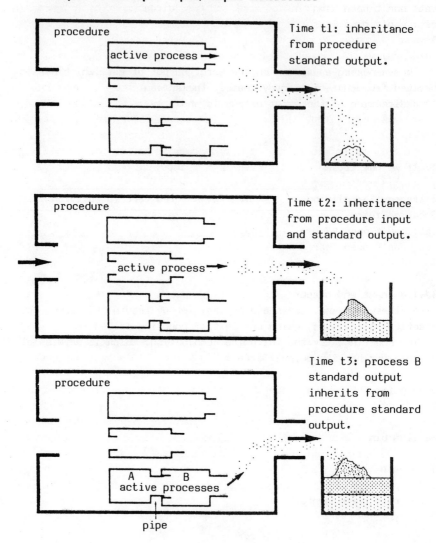

Time t1: inheritance from procedure standard output.

Time t2: inheritance from procedure input and standard output.

Time t3: process B standard output inherits from procedure standard output.

procedure

active process →

procedure

active process →

procedure

A ⌐ B
active processes

pipe

17.2 Filter

Viewed externally, **counting** reads at its standard input and writes to its standard output. It is a filter, in the UNIX sense, and can therefore be integrated within a pipe.

```
$ rev < kingjohn | counting | lpr
$
```

Here, **rev** inverts the **kingjohn** file line by line, writes to its standard output that is connected to the standard input of **counting**, which in turn outputs to its standard output. The latter is connected to the standard input of the spooler, which will give the usual result (4 lines) via the printer.

In more general terms, each procedure that reads at its standard input and writes to its standard output is a filter. This applies whatever the position in the procedure of the read process at the free standard input, of the write process(es) at the free standard output(s), the number of working files created, etc.

We have therefore seen that a procedure is no different from a 'pure' program, insofar as standard input/outputs are concerned. Hence their importance in the toolkit that the shell provides, and the need to think about problems (or break them down) in terms of independent modules that communicate with one another via their standard input/outputs.

17.3 Notes
We have examined multiple inheritances more in the interests of completeness than for their practical usefulness. Multiple input inheritance can be eliminated straight away, as it is virtually impossible.

On the other hand, multiple output inheritance is technically possible, but it must be used prudently. The following points should be borne in mind:
- if the successive writes result from different processing, the resultant output will be heterogeneous. The file will be more or less structured, but the elements or items will not all be of the same kind. The standard UNIX tools will no longer be able to handle such files conveniently. It would be better to tackle this type of problem with distinct files.
- if the resultant output is homogeneous, why write it several times?

17.4 Summary
A procedure has the same standard input/outputs as a 'pure' program. They are redirected in the same way.

```
procedure > file
procedure | process
procedure < file
process   | procedure
procedure 2> file
```

The effect of these redirections to the standard input/outputs of the processes internal to the procedure can be summarised as follows:

Standard inputs, outputs and error outputs, that are unassigned explicitly in a procedure, inherit respectively from those of the procedure.

18 Input and output on the spot

18.0 Session aim

Up until now, we have been able to (re)direct the standard input/
outputs to
- the keyboard or the screen (often by default)
- a file
- the input or output of other processes (pipe)

We shall now study two other possibilities.

18.1 Here document

We can regard the here document as a redirection of the standard input of a process to an area of the procedure itself.
    If the **birds** file contains the following

```
Cuckoos lead Bohemian lives,
They fail as husbands and as wives,
And so they cynically disparage
Everybody else's marriage
```

the command

```
$ grep "ives" < birds                    = gives
Cuckoos lead Bohemian lives,
They fail as husbands and as wives,
$
```

If we now create the following procedure, called **inives**

```
grep "ives" <<!
Cuckoos lead Bohemian lives,
They fail as husbands and as wives,
And so they cynically disparage
Everybody else's marriage
!
```

and execute it

```
$ inives                          = also gives
Cuckoos lead Bohemian lives,
They fail as husbands and as wives,
$
```

What has happened? The standard input of **grep** has been redirected to the area that begins at the line following that which includes <<! and ends at !

This area is called a here document. The ! is just an example here; it can be any string of characters, for example

```
$ grep ag << line
> Cuckoos lead Bohemian lives,
> They fail as husbands and as wives,
> And so they cynically disparage
> Everybody else's marriage
> line
And so they cynically disparage
Everybody else's marriage
$
```

grep will extract all the lines containing and lying between << line and > line.

The here document is used to put a heading on a file

```
cat - <<head  chapter | nroff -ms
.pl 45
.po 11
.ll 44
head
```

In a procedure, this sequence inserts in front of the file **chapter** instructions for **nroff. cat** concatenates its standard input in order, symbolised by the hyphen, with the file chapter. The standard input of **cat** being redirected to the here document, **nroff** recovers the above instructions, then the file **chapter.**

18.2 Command substitution

We can consider command substitution to be an 'on-the-spot' re-direction of the standard output of a process, at the very place where the process is mentioned.

We create the procedure **RLS**

echo "Blows the wind today, `date`, and the sun and the rain are flying"

the process **date** is written between left-sloping quote marks (or grave accents).

If we execute **RLS**

$ RLS   = gives
Blows the wind today, Wed 27 14:40:57 BST 1986,
                              and the sun and the rain are flying
$

Since **echo** repeats at its standard output what it is given as parameter, everything has occurred just as if **RLS** had contained

echo "Blows the wind today, Wed Aug 27 14:40:57 BST 1986,
      and the sun and the rain are flying"

In other words, at the precise position of **date**, the standard output of the process **date** has been substituted.

A complete pipeline can be placed within left-sloping quotes. Let us try the following pipeline (without using procedures)

$ ls | wc -1   = the reply could be
      5
$

Here **ls** lists the files of the current directory, one to a line, at its standard output, which is connected to **wc** which counts the number of lines read to its standard output.

We now try, again without using procedures

$ echo the directory contains `ls | wc -1` files
the directory contains 5 files   = reply
$

The 'final' standard output, that of **wc**, is the one that has been redirected on the spot. So, we must imagine that whatever is between the left-sloping quotes will give the standard output of the command (or pipeline, or more generally process). Command substitution makes it possible for example to pass as a parameter of a process B the standard output of another process A; in fact, it is possible to pass a large number of parameters to a process, many more than could be done manually (a hundred or more). As a result, to a certain

extent, the pipe technique and that of command substitution com-
plement one another.

```
process_A | process_B              = pipe method

process_B `process_A`              = substitution
```

   Command substitution is frequently used in shell programming,
especially for assigning shell variables. But this will be discussed
in the next session.

18.3 Summary
We have examined

```
here document:
process <<string
.

.
string
command substitution:
 process
```

19 Parameters and procedures

19.0 Session aim
We shall learn how to create procedure parameters, by means of shell positional variables.

19.1 Assigning parameters to a procedure
With our current knowledge, we can already imagine quite subtle input/output procedures, but they are still 'fixed' procedures. The only means of communication with the procedure is the standard input/output pair. Let us take the example of the following procedure **collection**

```
ls odes | pr -t -11 -3 | cat aunt -
```

The directory **odes** is placed in three columns on one-line pages (-11 forces the placement in columns when there is little data, see the utility **pr**). The standard output of **pr** is connected to **cat**, which will concatenate in order the **aunt** file and the work of **pr** read at its standard input (the dash -).

If we execute **collection**

```
$ collection
        Odes of my Aunt
Dreams              First_longing       His_name
Landscape           Morning             My_childhood
Nightmare           Promenade           Regrets
The_clouds          Thine
$
```

If **collection** saves us keying (and programming), we are nevertheless saddled with this heading and the three columns. But the idea of having to edit as many procedures as there are possible page displays comes as a shock. Better to follow the good example of producing only one procedure, with parameters. How are parameters passed? In the same way as a number of the commands that we have already reviewed, such as **echo, pr,** etc. The parameters follow the

procedure   name,   separated   by one or more spaces, something of the
form

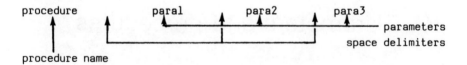

procedure name

In our case, suppose we wanted to pass as a parameter the number
of columns in **collection**. If we give this new version of collection
the name **collectionp**, its call will appear as

collectionp 4

Here, the display was to be in 4 columns.

Let us now look behind the scenes to see how the specified
parameters are recovered when the procedure is called.

The parameters are accessible as positional variables; that is,
variables located by their position (first, second, etc) in the command line when the procedure call is made.

Here is the listing of **collectionp**:

ls odes | pr -t -ll -$1 | cat aunt -

$1 represents the value of the first rank positional variable.
When the command is initiated

$ collectionp 4

the shell will replace **$1** with its value, here 4, then it will exe-
cute the pipeline. It is as though there had been

ls odes | pr -t -ll -4 | cat aunt -

and we shall then obtain

        Odes of my Aunt
Dreams   First_longing   His_name   Landscape
Morning   My_childhood   Nightmare   Promenade
Regrets   The_clouds   Thine

Here we only have a single argument. We could have had several,
which would have been accessed via **$1**, **$2**, **$3**, etc.

The general case can therefore be shown as

procedure	para1	para2	para3	...
	1	2	3	rank of
				positional
	$1	$2	$3	variables
				access to value
				of arguments

We are not limited to strictly numeric arguments, as in **collect-ionp.** More generally, arguments can be strings of characters, bounded by a delimiter character (a space, at the moment). The positional variables **1, 2, ...** are string variables; their value is a character string.

For example, take the following procedure **extract**

```
echo first argument value : $1
echo second argument value : $2
echo third argument    value : $3
echo $1, $3 and $2, the Good Samaritan
```

If we enter the command

```
$ extract Joseph Booz Ruth                 = gives
first argument value : Joseph
second argument value : Booz
third argument value : Ruth
Joseph, Ruth and Booz, the Good Samaritan
$
```

The corresponding parameter value is substituted for each **$1, $2,** etc encountered. This substitution takes place at the precise location of **$1**, etc, whatever the position and whatever the variable value. A positional variable might correspond to a directory name, and you might see the following appear in the procedure, for example

```
cd $1
```

The argument delimiter character (here a space) is obviously essential; if missing, there would be a fusion between arguments or with the name of the procedure itself.

Try

```
$collectionp4                     = gives
collectionp4: not found
$
```

This is because the procedure **collectionp4** does not exist.

extract expects three arguments. What happens if only two are supplied?

```
$ extract Joseph Ruth                    = gives
first argument value : Joseph
second argument value : Ruth
third argument value :
Joseph, and Ruth, the Good Samaritan
$
```

$3 is invisible, because it has not been possible to assign any value to variable 3, which has the value of an empty string. Unassigned positional variables have this value.

In this example, the procedure has been able to execute to the end, even though incorrectly. This is because **echo** is not very demanding. This is rarely the case; the shell exercises no control on the number of parameters expected by the procedure; it assigns a positional variable to each argument present at the time of the command. Without taking special precautions, there is no way of knowing which is the missing argument.

19.2 How many parameters?

It is now the time to concern ourselves with the number of arguments that we can handle and to present two special variables that are relevant.

19.2.1 Number of arguments

The number of arguments passed to a procedure is obtained by **$#**. Take the following procedure **narg**

```
echo there are $# arguments
```

We execute **narg**

```
$ narg a b c
there are 3 arguments
$ narg
there are 0 arguments
$ narg As those move easiest who have learned to dance
there are 9 arguments
$
```

We can access up to nine arguments in a procedure, from **$1** to **$9**. More exactly, **$1** to **$9** constitute a window of nine arguments, from a possibly longer list.

19.2.2 Beyond the nine arguments
There are two ways of accessing arguments in their totality. The first is by designating the totality of the arguments globally, by means of another special variable, **$***. Let us alter **narg** to obtain

```
there are $# arguments
echo I list them all at once :
echo $*
```

Try

```
$narg The curfew tolls the knell of parting day
there are 8 arguments
I list them all at once :
The curfew tolls the knell of parting day
$
```

Nothing particularly new yet, but then

```
$ narg a b c d e f g h i j k
there are 11 arguments
I list them all at once :
a b c d e f g h i j k
$
```

Everywhere that **$*** is specified, the shell will substitute for it the totality of the arguments, in their order of appearance to the command, with a space between each of them.

The second way of accessing arguments in their totality is by shifting the windowing of the 'nine' by means of the internal command **shift**. This command shifts each positional variable by one slot. Suppose we create the procedure **deca**, as follows

```
echo $# arguments as follows :
echo $* echo 1 2 and 9 : $1 $2 $9
shift
echo after a shift
echo $# arguments as follows :
echo $*
echo 1 2 and 9 : $1 $2 $9
```

   If we try it

```
$ deca a b c d e f g h i j k
11 arguments as follows :
a b c d e f g h i j k
1 2 and 9 : a b i
after a shift
10 arguments as follows :
b c d e f g h i j k
1 2 and 9 : b c j
$
```

   shift therefore has several effects: the former **$2** is now **$1**, the former **$3** has become **$2**, etc and the former **$10** is now accessible by **$9**. The number of arguments **$#** has been decreased by one.

   Now, the global list **$*** no longer includes the old **$1**, which has become inaccessible.

```
procedure   X   X   X   X   X  //   X   X   X ....
           $1  $2  $3  $4  $5  //  $9
           $1  $2  $3  $4  //  $8  $9         = after shift
```

19.3 Some further details

Maximum number of arguments:
It is difficult to state a precise value. The exact limit is a number of bytes (or characters), usually 5120, which is almost 'infinite' (it is no longer a small file).

Special variables:
We have already seen some of these: number of arguments (**$#**), total arguments (**$***). There are others, such as the positional variable **0** (zero). As its rank indicates, it precedes that of rank 1, and thus contains the name of the procedure itself. (Try introducing an **echo** **$0** into one of our procedures.)

   We shall meet some others later which are useful for more complex procedures than the ones we have seen so far.

19.4 Range of positional variables
Variables **0**, 1, 2, ... and the special values **$#** and **$*** are only recognised within the called procedure. These are local variables which come into being when the parametered procedure is called and die with it. In other words, every called procedure has its own set

of variables **0**, **1**, ... **#** and *****, which has nothing do with any other possible procedures. Let us look at the case of two nested procedures that we met in session 16.

First we create the calling procedure **call.1**:

```
echo I am $0
echo here are my $# arguments :
echo the first : $1
echo all : $*
echo call of call.2
call.2 A B
echo return to $0
echo there are still $# arguments
echo here they are : $*
```

and the called procedure **call.2**:

```
echo I am $0
echo here are my $# arguments
echo the first : $1
echo all : $*
```

The next command:

```
$ call.1 x y z
I am call.1
here are my 3 arguments :
the first : x
all : x y z
call of call.2
I am call.2
here are my 2 arguments :
the first : A
all : A B
return to call.1
there are still 3 arguments
here they are : x y z
$
```

19.5 Explicit assignment of positional variables

We have seen that the positional variables 1, 2, etc are loaded on procedure call by the values of the current arguments. It is also possible to assign values explicitly to these variables, within the procedure, by the internal command **set**.

This command assigns its arguments, in order, to the positional variables.

We shall create the procedure **st**

```
echo $# arguments
echo the first : $1
echo all : $*
set Down a road that is Martian red
echo after set
echo $# arguments
echo the first : $1
echo all : $*
```

and enter:

```
$ st Gully Foyle is my name
5 arguments
the first : Gully
all : Gully Foyle is my name
after set
7 arguments
the first : Down
all : Down a road that is Martian red
$
```

The positional variables and the number of arguments have been changed. The preceding values are lost.

This command is very useful for accessing one argument from a sequence of arguments. Suppose we wanted to access the month from the current year. The command **date** gives us this, but it is included in the sequence

```
Thur Aug 27 18:11:03 BST 1986
```

The answer is to use the command **set** `date`. After the command substitution, it is as though we have the following

```
set Thur Aug 28 18:11:03     ...         = arguments accessible
                                          = by

     $1  $2  $3          .....
```
so the name of the month is given by **$2**.
```
$ cat > month << !
> set `date`
> echo "This month is" $2
> !
```

```
$ chmod +x month
$ month
This month is Aug
$
```

In other words, **set** is a simple means of splitting up any chain into a set of positional variables.

19.6 Notes

We shall leave things there for the moment. The main thing to re-member is that we are not restricted to nine arguments; on the contrary, as we said in session 18, in many cases we shall have a much larger number of parameters, especially when the arguments are specified by command substitution of a process.

Take the following procedure **catal:**

```
echo this work contains $# poems
echo title of second : $2
```

The command gives

```
$ catal `ls odes`
this work contains 11 poems
title of second : First_longing
$
```

As we have seen in session 18, we have to imagine between the left-sloping quotes of the command substitution the result of **ls odes,** the listing of the directory **odes.** In procedure **catal,** we therefore only see a simple list of arguments; it does not make any difference whether this list was entered manually or by command substitution.

19.7 Summary

The parameters of a procedure are specified on the command line, after the name of the procedure itself.

```
procedure    paral    para2    ...
```

In the procedure, each parameter has assigned to it a positional variable string.

procedure	para1	para2	para3	...	= command
0	1	2	3		= assigned variable
$0	$1	$2	$3		= access to value of
					= parameters

Nine parameters can be accessed by their $ values, but there can be many more of them.

Values of special variables

$#   total number of arguments
$*   the set of all arguments

Internal shell commands

shift   has the following effects

- $* no longer includes the former $1, which is lost
- positional variables are shifted one slot: $2 becomes $1, etc
- the total $# is decremented by 1

set   (re)assigns positional variables and the special variables # and *.

20 Shell variables

20.0 Session aim
Here we shall examine how the shell can manipulate variables, just like a high-level language such as Fortran, C or BASIC.

20.1 Some general points
We shall see how the positional variables discussed in previous sessions are but a particular case of a shell variable.
- The name of a shell variable is a string of characters that always starts with a letter. For example

book

- Shell variables are string variables.
- The contents of a shell variable are obtained by inserting **$** in front of its name. For example

$book

20.2 Assigning a variable: the = operator
If we position ourselves at the terminal and confirm that we have the **$** request symbol on our screen, we can then key the following (note, no space around the = sign).

```
$ book=poems
$
```

Control is handed back. We have just created a shell variable called **book** and assigned it the value **poems**. It is important to omit spaces before or after the =, or the shell will confuse it with a command to search for an executable file. For example,

```
$ book =poems                              = gives
book : not found
$
```

163

(Unless, of course, there is such a file.)

We now check what **book** contains. **echo** is   the   command   to   use, since it repeats what it is given as argument.

```
$ echo $book
poems
$
```

Just as with positional variables, the shell substitutes the value of **book** at the exact position where **$book** appears.

Any assignment overwrites a previous one:

```
$ book=ballads
$ echo $book
ballads
$ book=                             = empty string
$ echo $book                        = gives
                                    = nothing
$
```

Finally, every unknown variable contains an empty string:

```
$ echo $paperback                   = gives
                                    = nothing
$
```

20.3 First use

Shell variables can be used interactively, as abbreviations. Suppose
we need frequent access to a file, which for some obscure reason, is
not in our current directory. Say we are in this directory

```
$ pwd
/users/florence/hugo
$
```

and our file is called, using a complete pathname

```
/users/florence/juliette/letters/guernsey/vj.l
```

We could of course list this file by

```
$ cat ../juliette/letters/guernsey/vj.l    = giving
Guernsey, ce
$
```

But that is pretty tedious, after a while. We can create the following variable **L**

```
$ L=../juliette/letters/guernsey/vj.1
$
```

We can now use **L** in place of the name of our file.

```
$ cat $L
Guernsey, ce
$
```

Similarly,

```
$ nroff -ms < $L | lpr
$
```

will process this file with **nroff** and output the result via the printer.

This method of abbreviation is more often used for directory names. To stay with our example

```
$ L=../juliette/letters/guernsey
$
```

Then, the command

```
$ ls $L/vj*                              = gives
../juliette/letters/guernsey/vj.1
../juliette/letters/guernsey/vj.2
../juliette/letters/guernsey/vj.3
             .
             .
$
```

We have the list of all the files of **../juliette/** etc whose name begins with **vj**.

There is nothing to prevent our assigning a value to a shell variable using a command substitution of a process. For example

```
$ whatday=`date`
$                                       = control handed back
```

From what we already know about command substitution, the above is equivalent to

whatday=Thu Aug 28 09:56:00 BST 1986

    It is no surprise to find that

$echo it is $whatday
it is Thu Aug 28 09:56:00 BST 1986
$

    Something more interesting still can be seen in the next example.
Suppose we list the beginning of the file called **West_Wind** contained
in the directory **odes:**

$ cat odes/West_Wind
O wild West Wind, thou breath of Autumn's being,
Thou, from whose unseen presence the leaves dead
Are driven, like ghosts from an enchanter fleeing.
$

    We can assign a whole file to a variable:

$ West= cat odes/West_Wind   = hands back control
$

    The variable **West** now contains the whole of our file (this makes
it clear that it is a string variable).

$ echo $West
O wild West Wind, thou breath of Autumn's being, Thou, from whose
unseen presence the leaves dead Are driven, like ghosts from an
enchanter fleeing.
$

    Setting aside the problem of carriage returns, everything else is
there.
    It is often necessary for there to be much coming and going be-
tween two directories. One may contain 'sources' (material in Fortran, C, etc) of a program in the process of being written, together
with latest executable version of this program. The other may be the
'test' directory, containing test files. In such cases, it is
convenient to have two shell variables, one for each directory.
    Suppose we begin in the **test** directory.

```
$ pwd                                = gives
/users/espesser/operation
$ E=`pwd`                            = replace 'test'
$ T=/users/espesser/signal/synt      = replace source
$ cd $T
$ pwd                                = verify
$ /users/espesser/signal/synt
$ ex cvocal.c                        = alterations to source
            .                        = compile, etc
            .
$ cd $E                              = return to /operation
$ $T/cvocal < zone/a | writer        = test this version
Floating exception : core dumped     = bad error!
$ cd $T                              = we return
$ ed cvocal.c                        = to continue...
```

20.4 How to terminate a variable

We have seen how the value of a variable is substituted at the precise place where it is called by the **$**. For example, if

```
$ RHYME=ney
$ echo "They took some ho$RHYME, and plenty of mo$RHYME"
They took some honey, and plenty of money
$
```

You should use braces to separate the variable from surrounding text. This is essential if a letter or a number immediately follows the variable. For example

```
$ echo "That film was one of Jimmy Cag$RHYMEs"
That film was one of Jimmy Cag
$ echo "That film was one of Jimmy Cag${RHYME}s"
That film was one of Jimmy Cagneys
```

The first example fails, as the shell is using a variable called **RHYMEs**, which is assumed to be unassigned, and therefore empty.

20.5 Default substitution of shell variables

We know that an unassigned variable has the value of an empty string. It is possible to obtain a default substitution in such cases.

Take the shell variable **writer**, unassigned, and try the sequence

```
$ echo $writer                          = gives
                                        = empty
$ echo ${writer-byron}                  = gives
byron
$
```

The string **byron** has been substituted by default for the value of the variable **writer.** By contrast

```
$ writer=Keats                          = assignment
$ echo ${writer-Byron}                  = gives
Keats
$
```

Here, **writer** has been assigned a value; therefore there is no default substitution.

Writing

```
$ var-string
```

where the variable **var** is unassigned, allows the string specified after the hyphen to be substituted for it. (There are two other possible default actions for shell variables.)

These techniques also apply to positional shell variables, and are in fact mainly used in a procedure, in order to replace missing arguments.

20.6 Use in procedures

Shell variables are used in a procedure in order to store an intermediate result and then call it subsequently. Assignment by command substitution is therefore used extensively. In order to take full advantage of the possibilities provided by the shell, it is important to be provided with processes that make the best use of their standard input/outputs. This is certainly true of the UNIX utility programs.

We shall here summarise the utility **expr**, which we shall need. It evaluates the logical or arithmetic expression that is passed to it as argument, and gives the result at its standard output. For example

```
$ expr 5 - 3
2
$
```

Pay attention to the essential spaces before and after the minus sign (and other operators, such as +, /, *).

A variable can thus be incremented by 1

```
$ m=7                              = 1
$ m= `expr $m + 1`                 = 2
$ echo $m                          = gives
8
$
```

Here, in line 1 the initial value of **m** is 7. In line 2 the shell replaces **$m** with its value (it evaluates **$m**), namely 7. Then it executes the command, that is, **expr** 7 + 1, redirecting to the standard output. Finally, **m** is assigned what is found to the right of the =, namely 8.

Of course, arithmetic operators are only valid for strictly numeric variables.

Suppose we now create the following procedure **stylug**:

```
poem=$1                            = 1
set `wc <$poem`                    = 2
avword= `expr $2 / $1`             = 3
echo $poem consists of :
echo $1 lines, $2 words and $3 characters
echo that is an average of $avword words per line
```

What does **stylug** do? It functions with an argument, which is the name of the file containing a poem to be analysed. We shall examine this line by line.

line 1: copies **$1** (the file name) into the shell variable **poem**

line 2: a) the shell makes the command substitution: instead of **wc...** we have 3 numeric values: the number of lines, the number of words and the number of characters of the file that is passed as parameter.

b) **set** takes these 3 values as arguments, and assigns them to the positional variables 1, 2 and 3; **$1** now has the value of the number of lines in the file, which is why it was previously copied to **poem**. **$2** gives the number of words and **$3** the number of characters.

line 3: calculates the ratio of words to lines and places the average in variable **avword**.

subsequent lines: display the results.

echo, which you might have thought to be a rather useless utility, now comes into its own. It is the equivalent of the output instructions of many programming languages (print for BASIC, write for Fortran, etc).

Let us take the file **Tiger** to test **stylug**:

Tiger, Tiger, burning bright
In the forests of the night,
What immortal hand, or eye,
Could frame thy fearful symmetry?

```
$ stylug Tiger
Tiger consists of :
4 lines, 20 words and 121 characters
that is an average of 5 words per line
$
```

20.7 Range of shell variables

As with the positional variables that we met in session 19, shell variables are only recognised within the procedure in which they appear. For example

```
$ avword=122
$ stylug Tiger
Tiger consists of :
4 lines, 20 words and 121 characters
that is an average of 5 words per line
$ echo $avword
122
$
```

The variable **avword** assigned before the calling of **stylug** has nothing to do with the one that exists within **stylug**.

Shell variables are local variables, which live for as long as the procedure in which they appear.

As for **avword**, it will hold its value until the next assignation; it ceases to exist when you log off.

20.8 Assigning variables: internal command read

We shall consider the following procedure **act**:

```
read family forename1
echo "forename(s) :" $forename1
echo surname : $family
```

and the following file **register**:

```
SHELLEY Percy Bysshe
KEATS John
```

This gives

```
$ act < register
forename(s) : Percy Bysshe
surname : SHELLEY
$
```

    read has read at the standard input of the procedure a line of the file register. The first word, SHELLEY, has been placed in the first variable, **family**, and the remainder of the line in the variable **forename1**.

    More generally speaking, **read** reads a single line at a time at the standard input of the procedure in which it is included. The successive words in this line are placed in order in the variables mentioned, with any remaining words being placed in the last variable.

    If we make this alteration to **act:**

```
read family forename1 forename2
echo "forename(s) :" $forename1
echo "forename(s) :" $forename2
echo surname : $family
read family forename1 forename2
echo "forename(s) :" $forename1
echo "forename(s) :" $forename2
echo surname : $family
```

we get:

```
$ act < register
forename(s) : Percy
forename(s) : Bysshe
surname : SHELLEY
forename(s) : John
forename(s) :
surname : KEATS
$
```

    Here, since **read** has an additional variable, the two forenames can be located separately. The second **read** reads the next line of the file register.

    Note that **read** reads at the standard input of the procedure in which it is included, not its own standard input. **Read** is not a process, but an internal shell command (we shall meet others). Thus, it is not possible to write

read variable < file

20.9 Special variables
We have already seen

$#** (number of arguments), **$* (arguments globally).

There are many others. Here is **$$**, which gives the number of the process of the procedure in which it appears. For example, the following procedure **num:**

echo $$

$ num
$ 6460
$

6460 was the process identity number (PID) of the process **num** (see session 9.7 for PID); 6460 no longer exists since **num** is terminated.

The advantage of **$$** is as follows: a PID is unique (there is only one PID process at any given moment). **$$** thus serves to generate unique file names, which is useful in a multi-tasking, multi-user context like UNIX. Suppose that two processes (one or two users) each want to create a temporary working file in the same directory; it is better to give them names that are guaranteed to be different. A simple method of doing this is to add **$$** to the selected name. Here are some examples:

```
. . . > /tmp/provis$$          = creation and writing
.
. . . < /tmp/provis$$          = recover data

.
rm -f /tmp/*$$                 = clear out at end of procedure
```

The **/tmp** directory is in fact often used for temporary working files, and it is common to all users and processes.

20.10 Summary
The shell can manipulate string variables.

The name of a shell variable is a string of characters beginning
with a letter. For example

rhyme

The value of **rhyme** is given by

$rhyme
${rhyme}

- default substitution

${var-string}

- assignment:

rhyme=   = direct assignment

rhyme=`date`   = assignment by command substitution

read rhyme   = assignment by internal read command

read reads a line at the standard input of the procedure in which it
is included, and assigns in order a word of this line to each variable mentioned. The last variable contains the remainder of the
line.

21 Interpretation and neutralisation of special characters

21.0 Session aim
This is a tricky session, requiring close visual attention. We shall be learning how to master the mechanism for the interpretation of certain characters by the shell - such characters as spaces (or blanks), *, < and >, etc, that we have met on frequent occasions.

21.1 Special (meta)characters - their interpretation
We have met nearly all of the following:

- space (or blank)
this is a delimiter. In cases like the following, it helps the shell to access the different arguments

     command   argl   arg2   arg3   ...

- new-line
the return to a line has the same effect. It indicates the logical end of line (for example, a command line).

- semi-colon
it separates commands on a single line

$ ls ; date   = two distinct commands

- generic characters:
*   for any string
?   for a single character
[]   for a list of characters

- metacharacters for redirecting input/outputs:
left-sloping single primes   , >, >>, <, << and

- parentheses ()
for grouping commands.

174

- ampersand **&**
for initiating a background command.

21.2 Neutralisation of a character
There are occasions when the interpretation (or evaluation) of these
special characters is inconvenient. If you want to specify a command
that extends over more than one line on the screen, how do you avoid
the shell evaluating a Return? We have already seen how, in fact, by
inserting a backslash at the end of the line to indicate continua-
tion.

```
$ ls \
> -1                                    = secondary call
  .   .   .
$                                       = equivalent to
$ ls -1
  .   .   .
$
```

   The backslash has cancelled the interpretation of the Return.
   The more usual function of the backslash is to cancel the interpretation of the character that immediately follows it. For example

```
$ ls \*                                 = gives
* not found                             = no file called *
$
```

or, again

```
$ poet=john
$ echo $poet
john                                    = gives
$ echo \$poet                           = do not confuse
$poet                                   = the $s
$
```

Another example

```
$ ls \; date                            = gives
; not found
date not found
$
```

   Here, the ; is cancelled by the backslash. The shell only 'under-
stands' one command, that is, **ls** with two arguments ; and **date**,

which are both taken to be file names. Hence the response (always assuming that there is no file called **date** in your current directory).

   The backslash will also cancel itself

```
$ echo the \\ cancels itself            = gives
the \ cancels itself
$
```

   Neutralisation is essential in order to be able to pass arguments to certain utilities; as with **expr**, for example.
   For

```
$ expr 4 + 11                           = gives
15
$
```

there is no problem; but for

```
$ expr 444 * 2                          = gives
syntax error
$
```

   Here, the shell proceeded immediately to evaluate the generic character *****, replacing it with all the file names in the current directory, which confused **expr**. The answer is straightforward

```
$ expr 444 \* 2                         = gives
888
$
```

In this way, **expr** gets what belongs to it, the operator *****.

21.3 Neutralisation of a string
The backslash only works for a single character; it has to be repeated for each metacharacter that is to be neutralised.

```
$ echo \*\*\>                           = gives
**>
$
```

which is hardly useful.

You can neutralise a complete string by placing it within single quote marks

```
$ echo '***>'                          = gives
***>
$
```

Here is a more interesting example:

```
$ line='To boldly go where no man has gone before'
$ echo $line                           = gives
To boldly go where no man has gone before
$
```

The quotes have neutralised the spaces between the words, so that they have not been interpreted as delimiters; so the string is taken to be a unique variable.

Without the quotes, the response would be:

```
$ line=To boldly go where no man has gone before
boldly: not found
$
```

Here, the shell has looked for a file called **boldly** to execute. In fact our command line corresponds to a more advanced form of process initiation by the shell.

The use of quote marks has important consequences when passing arguments to a procedure.

If we recreate the following **narg** procedure:

```
echo $0 has $# arguments
echo the first : $1
echo the second : $2
echo the third : $3
echo all : $*
```

and key in

```
$ narg These are the voyages of the starship Enterprise
narg has 8 arguments
the first : These
the second : are
the third : the
all : These are the voyages of the starship Enterprise
```

If we instead type

```
$ narg These 'are the voyages' 'of the starship' Enterprise
narg has 4 arguments
the first : These
the second : are the voyages
the third : of the starship
all : These are the voyages of the starship Enterprise
```

What is shown between the quote marks constitutes a single string variable, and is therefore taken as a unique argument.

All metacharacters are neutralised when placed between quotes, including the backslash. The only exception is the quote mark itself; it is interpreted as the end of neutralisation. This means that is is not possible to nest pairs of quotes. For example

```
$ echo '`date` '                    = gives
`date`
$
```

On close examination of the quotes, it will be noted that a command substitution has been neutralised. Fortunately, this is not very useful.

Single quotes are often used to neutralise a string passed as an argument to certain utilities, like **grep** or **sed.** They have their own set of metacharacters and generic characters (the same as **ex/ed**), that resemble that of the shell, but with different meanings!

We will return to the verse that we used for the **stylug** procedure in session 20.

```
Tiger, Tiger, burning bright
In the forests of the night,
What immortal hand, or eye,
Could frame thy fearful symmetry?
```

We want to extract all the lines including at least one word that ends with the letter d. The regular expression that describes this requirement for **grep** is as follows

```
[^ ].*d[ ,.]
```

Where
[^] means beginning of line or space
d means d
[,.] means a space, or a comma or a period.

The whole means, sort everything that
- begins with a new line or a blank,   followed by
- anything,   followed by
- d,   followed by
- a blank or a comma or a period.

The assumption is therefore that a word is preceded by a blank or
a new line, and is followed by a blank, a comma or a period.
   We key this

```
$ grep '[^ ].*d[ ,.]' < Tiger
What immortal hand, or eye,
Could frame thy fearful symmetry?
```

Here, it is essential to include the command between quotes.
Better not try it without.

21.4 Partial neutralisation

We will complicate things a little more. We no longer simply want to
obtain the words ending in **d**, but obtain any string at the end of a
word. We shall therefore need to create a filter type procedure,
with a single argument, that is, the string to be searched for. This
procedure will therefore contain

```
grep '[^ ].*$l[ ,.]'
```

On reflection, this will not work. The **$1**, which symbolises our
argument (the end string that we seek), will not be evaluated by the
shell, because it is between quotes. But, we cannot remove the single quotes.
   This is where we can use the double quotes instead. We create the
final procedure, which contains

```
grep "[^ ].*$l[ ,.]"
```

```
$ final ht < Tiger                = gives
Tiger, Tiger, burning bright
In the forests of the night,      = two lines having at least one
                                    word ending in "ht"; note that
                                    there must be a space after
                                    "bright", rather than the "end-
                                    of-line" character .. which is
                                    unaccounted for in 'final'
```

When placed between double quotes, all special characters are neutralised, except **$ ' ** and " (as for single quotes, double quotes cannot neutralise themselves).

Operations that can be carried within double quotes are the evaluation of shell variables and command substitutions; however, the expansion of generic characters and the interpretation of blanks cannot.

We will look at this with procedure **narg** and two shell variables:

```
$ line1='I am content'
$ line2=I do not care'
$ narg '$line1 $line2'
narg has 1 arguments
the first : $line1 $line2
the second :
the third :
all : $line1 $line2
```

This was just a small reminder of the effect of the quotes which neutralise everything. Now

```
$ narg "$line1" "$line2"              = gives
narg has 2 arguments
the first : I am content
the second : I do not care
the third :
all : I am content I do not care
$
```

The two variables have been evaluated, but not the blanks included in **line1** and **line2**. There are only two arguments, in contrast to:

```
$ narg $line1 $line2              = which gives
narg has 7 arguments
the first : I
the second : am
the third : content
all : I am content I do not care
$
```

which contains an integrated interpretation.

The double quotes allow one to carry out subtle pieces of evaluation like:

```
$ echo "$line1\$line2"
I am content $line2
$
```

Here, the backslash is not neutralised betwen the double quotes, so it was able to neutralise the **$.**

21.5 Evaluation

21.5.1 Order of evaluation
We have made much use of the terms evaluation, interpretation of variables, of special characters, etc. It is now time to examine the order in which they function.

Before executing a command, the shell does the following, in order:

a) substitution of variables (evaluation of the **$**)
b) command substitution (evaluation of quotes)
c) interpretation of blanks (or spaces, new-line). After a) and b), the resultant characters are separated by delimiters
d) evaluation of generic characters: ***, [], ?** Each file name is a separate argument
e) execute the command.

On a first reading, the reader might wish to pass over the next two sections.

21.5.2 Level of evaluation
The shell has only one level of evaluation. But what do we mean by that? Suppose that:

```
$ V2=Herge                        = gives
$ V1='$V2'
$ echo $V1
$V2
$
```

The shell has only evaluated **V1** 'once'. At the first level, **V1** has the value **$V2**; the shell has not evaluated this **$V2** in turn.

The same applies to commands like:

```
$ C='date |wc'                    = gives
$ $C
date|wc: not found
$
```

The shell evaluates **$C,** but stops there.

21.5.3 Internal command: eval
This internal command solves problems of evaluation at several levels.

   eval evaluates its arguments, like every command, and transmits the result to the shell, which reads it, evaluates it in turn itself, and executes the resultant command.

   If we go back to our two variables **V1** and **V2:**

```
$ eval echo $V1                          = gives
Herge
$
```

   In fact, **eval** carries out a first interpretation and gives:

```
echo $V2
```

   This result is transmitted to the shell, which interprets it as:

```
echo Herge
```

and executes it.

   The same goes for our variable **C:**

```
$ eval $C                                = gives
     1       6       29                   = the last number may vary
$
```

   It is possible to place several **eval** in sequence, with each evaluating at one level and passing the result to the next.

21.6 Notes
The complex problems of neutralisation and evaluation are rare for normal programming in the shell. Often, the use of single or double quotes solves the problem. In every case, neutralisation is more unreadable than difficult.

21.7 Summary
`\` neutralises any special character that follows it
`'...'` any string between single quotes is neutralised, except `'`
`"..."` any string between double quotes is neutralised, except **$ ' \ "**

The shell only evaluates at one level.
eval offers another evaluation level.

22 Control structures

22.0 Session aim

The procedures that we have examined so far have only executed sequentially. However, the shell can also handle loops, conditional branches and multiple branches, just like a conventional algorithmic language.

22.1 Multiple branch: case

We will take the following procedure, called **poems**

```
case $1 in
byron) echo on `date`
       echo poems available; ls odes | pr -t -3 -ll
       ;;
keats) echo in course of composition ;;
*) echo author unknown ;;
esac
```

```
$ poems keats                          = gives
in course of composition
$ poems byron
on Sun Oct 19 14:49:46 BST 1986
poems available
Don_Juan                Lara                    Napoleon_Bonaparte
Parisina                Prometheus              Saul
Stanza_to_Augusta       The_Dream               Versicles
$ poems armitage
author unknown
$
```

The shell has compared **$1** in succession with each of the three patterns mentioned in the 'case':

byron keats and 'anyone', represented by *

When there is a match, the corresponding list of commands is executed.

The general form of the multiple branch is as follows:

```
case  string  in
pattern) list of commands ;;
pattern) list of commands ;;
    .
    .
pattern) list of commands ;;
esac
```

The shell compares the string in order with each pattern specified between **case** and **esac**. At the first match, the list of commands
found between the **)** and the **;;** is executed. The system then jumps to
the end of **case**, represented by **esac** (case inverted).

A list of commands is a sequence of one or more commands separated or terminated by a **;** or a line return. This list can be empty.

The range of comparisons that can be made is extensive; for
example, variables, command substitutions and the generic characters
*, **?** and **[]** can appear in the patterns. Since the asterisk matches
any string, it often appears as the last pattern in a **case**, in order
to handle unforeseen cases.

The shell works through the patterns in their order of appearance. There is no control to see if several patterns match the
string. If we had edited **poems** as follows:

```
case $1 in
*) echo author unknown ;;
byron) echo on `date`
       echo poems available; ls odes | pr -t -3 -11
       ;;
keats) echo in course of composition ;;
esac
$ poems keats
author unknown
$
```

poems will now always give us author unknown.

The use of generic characters allows some flexibility in the comparisons. Suppose we alter the procedure **poems** to obtain:

```
case $1 in
*byron*) echo on `date`
         echo poems available; ls odes   pr -t -3 -11
```

```
      ;;
*keats*) echo in course of composition ;;
*) echo author unknown ;;
esac
```

this will for example allow

```
$ poems 'lord byron'                    = gives
on Sun Oct 19 14:51:56 BST 1986 poems available
Don_Juan                  Lara                  Napoleon_Bonaparte
Parisina                  Prometheus            Saul
Stanza_to_Augusta         The_Dream             Versicles
$
```

because we have allowed any strings before and after **byron**. Note that the neutralisation is essential so that **lord byron** becomes a single variable.

We will take another example, as follows:

```
case $1 in
*[A-z]*) echo  $1 non numeric ;;
*) echo $1 numeric ;;
esac
```

```
$ test_num 1111
1111 numeric
$ test_num jam
jam non mumeric
$ test_num 11A1
11A1 non numeric
$ test_num 111-333
111-333 numeric
$
```

This can test if the variable **$1** is numeric or not. ***[A-z]*** will match with any string containing at least one letter of the alphabet.

Therefore there is a good chance that other cases, represented by *****, will be purely numeric.

Note that the expansion of the generic characters *****, **[]** and **?** is in a broader pattern. You no longer generate file names, but strings of normal characters.

It is also possible to have alternative choices in the pattern. Suppose we alter the **poems** procedure:

```
case $1 in
*byron* | *Byron | *BYRON* ) echo on `date`
      echo poems available; ls odes | pr -t -3 -ll
      ;;
*keats*) echo in course of composition ;;
*) echo author unknown ;;
esac
```

There will be a match if **$1** contains **byron** or **Byron** or **BYRON.** The vertical bar (the same symbol as for pipes) is used here to separate the choices.

The normal neutralisation rules are valid in the patterns:

```
case $1 in
'*byron*') . . .
```

is only recognised if **$1** literally has the value

```
*byron*
```

22.2 for loop
Take the following procedure, called **stylis:**

```
for poem in Don_Juan The_Dream Versicles
do
echo $poem belongs to Odes
done
echo task completed
```

If we execute:

```
$ stylis                              = gives
Don_Juan belongs to Odes
The_Dream belongs to Odes
Versicles belongs to Odes
task completed
$
```

The **for** loop has executed the command **echo** for each value of the variable **poem,** taken in succession from the list specified after the **in.**

The usual notation of a **for** loop is:

```
for variable in m1 m2 m3 ...
do
```

```
list of commands
done
```

The commands specified between the **do** and the **done** are executed for each value of the shell variable **variable.** On the first pass, **variable** has the value m1; on the second pass, variable has the value m2, and so on, until the list of arguments is exhausted. If the list is empty, the **for** loop does not execute.

Another name for this control structure is index repetition. The counting loops in Fortran, BASIC and C are only a particular example of this structure.

Of course, the list m1, m2, etc can be specified using all the techniques we have seen so far, especially by command substitution.

Suppose we change the **stylis** procedure:

```
for poem in  ls odes
do
echo analysis of $poem
stylug odes/$poem
done
echo task completed
```

The quotes contain the list of files in the **odes** directory. For each value of **poem,** that is, for each file of **odes, stylis** will execute:

```
echo analysis of $poem
stylug $poem
```

(**stylug** was introduced in session 20.)

The list of **for** loop-index values can also be constructed from the positional variable values **1, 2,** etc.

If we simply alter the first line of **stylis** to obtain:

```
for poem in $*
do
done
echo task completed
```

Then we could use **stylis** as follows:

```
$ stylis odes/The_Dream
analysis of odes/The_Dream
task completed
```

Since there was only one argument, there was only one value in the loop list, and therefore only one pass.

Another example:

```
$ stylis                           = no arguments
task completed
$
```

Here there is no argument, **$*** is an empty string; therefore, the **for** loop does not execute, and the structure executes the end of **stylis**.

In **stylis**, we could have written more simply:

```
for poem                          = equivalent to for poem in $*
do
done
```

$* is the default for the loop list; this is because, when combined with **case**, the **for** loop is frequently used to analyse a command and its arguments.

Although a digression, it is worth noting that the last version of the procedure **stylis** loops when called by **stylug**. It would have been interesting to preserve or process the results of **stylug** at each pass, in order to be able to find the average, for example. But, we cannot. Why? Suppose **stylug** gives us this, for example:

```
Versicles consists of :
12 lines, 48 words and 228 characters
that is an average of 4 words per line
```

It is now very difficult to extract from so much verbiage the information required for general statistics. On the other hand, if **stylug** only produced 4 values on one and the same line (like **wc**), we would have been able to access any of them easily by:

```
set `stylug`
```

(Then, **$1**, **$2**, **$3** and **$4** would give us the values that we wanted.)

This is just one example of where nicely presented listings are not necessarily the most useful; it also explains why the UNIX utilities are so concise. Choosing the more user friendly from **wc** and **stylug** might turn out to be a surprise. (If the output from **wc** appears too austere, create a procedure to supplement it.)

22.3 Summary

We have looked at two control structures:

multiple branch **case**

case string **in**
pattern) list of commands ;;
pattern) list of commands ;;
esac

for loop

for shell variable **in** list of strings
do
list of commands
done

23 Further control structures and reroutings

23.0 Session aim

We complete our study of control structures (**if-then-else, while** loops, etc).

We tackle standard reroutings (**exit, break** and **continue**) and reroutings from external events (**trap**).

23.1 Code for return from a process

This concept is now essential in order to understand the remaining control structures.

Every process ('pure' program or procedure) initiated by the shell ends by sending a return code to the shell. This is a numerical value that allows us to monitor the conditions for the execution of the process.

We shall not tackle the way in which a 'pure' program (written in C or Fortran, etc) transmits this return code to the shell. For those readers who have already programmed in C, it is the instruction exit(n) that sees to this, where n is the return code.

What is of interest at this point, is how to use this code.

23.1.1 Special variable return code

The shell variable **?** always contains the return code of the last command to be executed. For example

```
$ pwd
/users/moira
$ echo $?                              = gives
0
$                 .
```

By convention, the zero value means that execution of the process was normal (or correct); a non-zero value represents an anomaly or incorrect execution. Here is a way of remembering this

```
0    correct      cOrrect
1    incorrect     Incorrect
```

For example

```
$ cat non_exist                          = intentional error
non_exist: No such file or directory
$ echo $?
1
$
```

Because **cat** is unable to access **non_exist**, it returns 1 as code to the shell.

23.1.2 Internal command exit

How does a procedure communicate its return code to the shell?

First, it can be done implicitly. A procedure ends by sending as its return code the code of the last command executed.

We shall create the following procedure **status**. We have removed the output of the **cat**s by redirecting their output to the special file **/dev/null**, which disposes of unwanted data, like a dustbin. We thus only keep what is of interest to us.

```
cat status > /dev/null
echo first return : $?
echo with error
cat non_exist  > /dev/null 2> /dev/null
```

Now, execute

```
$ status                        = gives
first return : 0
with error
$ echo $?
1                               = status return
$
```

The return of **cat** has the value 1. It is also the code that the procedure **status** returns.

Secondly, the return code can be transmitted explicitly, using the internal command **exit**.

This command causes the current procedure to be abandoned; it is a rerouting or trap. Without arguments, the return code is that of the last command to be executed; with numeric argument (exclusively), **exit** takes this value as its return code.

If we alter **status** thus:

```
cat status > dev/null
echo first return : $?
exit
echo with error
cat non_exist  > /dev/null 2> /dev/null
```

Then

```
$ status                                = gives
first return : 0
$ echo $?                               = status return
0
$
```

status terminated with the command **exit** (its code is that of the last executed command, **echo** in this case).

If we alter **status** again:

```
cat status > /dev/null
echo first return : $?
echo with error
cat non_exist  > /dev/null 2> /dev/null
exit 2
```

We obtain:

```
$ status
first return : 0
with error
$ echo $?                                       = status return
2
$
```

Here we have specified the value of 2 as return code for the procedure status.

23.1.3 Use of return code

The value **$?** is used for every shell command result. Therefore, suppose that in a procedure **call1**, we call a procedure **call2** (an example of nested procedures). We could test the operation of **call2** by the following:

```
call2
case $? in
0) ;;                                          = normal, no problem
*) echo error on call2 ;exit 1 ;;             = abandon
esac
```

On receiving an abnormal return code from **call2**, execution of **call1** is abandoned, with a code return of 1.

23.2 test command

The **test** command evaluates the logical expression that is passed to it as argument, and sends a zero return code if it is true, or a non-zero code if it is false. For example

```
$ test 5 -eq 5                                = numerically equal?
$ echo $?
0                                             = true
$
$ test 12 -le 13                             = less than or equal?
$ echo $?
0                                             = true
$
$ x=Byron
$ y=Pope
$ test $x = $y                               = literally equal?
$ echo $?
1                                            = false
$
```

You will need to refer to the documentation on **test** to be aware of all the possible operators and options. However, here are a few that will be of use later.

```
test -s file
```

The return is 0 (true) if **file** exists and has a non-null length (s for string).

```
test -d file
```

The return is true if **file** exists and is a directory (d for directory).
- if not, the **else** branch is executed, here an error message.

test string

The return is true if **string** is not an empty string.
The existence of this command adds a further dimension to the
return code by allowing to become the keystone of the following two
control structures:

if then else
while

23.3 if then else structure
Suppose our directory **odes** is still intact. We will create the procedure **stock**:

```
if test -d $1
then
        echo $1 contains `ls $1 | wc -l` poems
else
        echo $1 is not a stock item
fi
```

We try it:

```
$ stock odes                                = gives
odes contains 9 poems
$
```

and

```
$ stock odes/The_Dream
odes/The_Dream is not a stock item
$
```

To explain: in the first case, the command **test -d $1** evaluated
as

```
test -d odes
```

returns a true status. **odes** is a non-empty directory. The **if** tests
this return code:
- if it is zero, the shell executes the **then** branch, here a simple
count of the elements in the directory.

What happens on the second call to **stock** is that **odes/The_Dream**
is not a directory.

The general form of the **if** branch is as follows:

```
if command-list-1
then command-list-2
else command-list-3
fi
```

If the return code of the last command in command-list-1 is zero (or true), the **then** branch is executed (command-list-2). If not, the **else** branch is executed (command-list-3).

Do not forget to terminate an 'if block' by **fi.**

The **else** branch is optional, which means that you can have:

```
if command-list-1
then command-list-2
fi
```

if is frequently used with the **test** process, but not solely. It is also used to ensure correct execution of a command. Taking again the example of the control process **call2** in the procedure **call1** (see 23.1.3), we could have written:

```
if call2
then ;                          = normal, nothing to be done
else echo error on call2;exit 1
fi
```

if structures can be nested, to obtain examples like:

```
if ...
then ...
    ...
    if ...
    then ...
    else ...
    fi
fi
```

In the case of **if** with multiple choices, like:

```
if ...
then ...
else if ...
    then ...
```

```
    else if ...
    ...
    etc ...
```

the **else if** can be replaced by **elif**:

```
if ...
then ...
elif ...
fi
```

23.4 while loop

Take the following procedure **count**:

```
m=1
while test $m -le $1
do
echo iteration $m
m=` expr $m + 1`
done
echo end of counting
```

and execute it:

```
$ count 3
iteration 1
iteration 2
iteration 3
end of counting
$
```

Here, at the start variable **m** is initialised to 1. **test $m -le $1** sends the shell a zero return code if **m** is less than or equal to **$1** (the counting argument, which has the value 3 here).

while tests this return code. If it is zero, because **m** is less than 3, the command list between **do** and **done** is executed. **m** is displayed, and incremented by 1, and the structure begins again at **while test**.

When **m** reaches 4, the return code from **test** will be non-zero. Now, the **while** loop is abandoned, and the structure jumps to after **done**.

The general form of the **while** loop is thus:

```
while command-list-1
do
command-list-2
done
```

    while tests the return code of the last command of command-list-1.

    If it is zero (or true), command-list-2 is executed, and the structure restarts at **while.**

    If not, the **while** loop is terminated.

    Here is another example. The internal command **read**, introduced in session 20, returns a non-zero code if it finds an end of file. So, a sequence of the form:

```
while read L
do
echo $L
. . .
done
```

displays a line of the standard input, continues the process (the dotted line) and restarts on the next line, for as long as the end of the file has not been reached. When it is reached, **read** returns a non-zero code, and the **while** is terminated.

    There is a symmetrical form of the **while** loop, namely the **until** loop. Its general format is:

```
until command-list-1
do
command-list-2
done
```

    Command-list-2 will be executed until the return code of the last command in command-list-1 is zero.

23.5 Rerouting
We have already seen the **exit** command, which abandons the procedure currently being executed.

23.5.1 break command
This command causes the **for** or **while** loop to be abandoned at the point where it is inserted. The procedure continues after the **done.**

Take the procedure **classify**:

```
for i
do
case $i
in
[A-Z]*) UPP="$UPP $i" ;:
[a-z]*) LOW="$LOW $i" ;;
[0-9]*) break ;;
*);;
esac
done
echo $LOW
echo $UPP
```

```
$ classify Oh! how many Sailors, how many Captains      = gives
how many how many
Oh! Sailors, Captains
$
```

but

```
$ classify Oh! how many Sailors, 8, how many Captains 3     = gives
how many
Oh! Sailors,
$
```

classify collects all the arguments starting with an upper case
letter into variable **UPP**; it collects all the arguments starting
with a lower case letter into variable **LOW**. It stops at the first
argument starting with a number.

Some further explanation of UPP="$UPP $i" would be helpful.
Between the double quotes, the variables are evaluated, but not the
space. UPP is concatenated with i, and the result stored in UPP. On
the first pass, UPP has the value of an empty string, i is Oh!; so
after assignment UPP has the value Oh!. On the next pass, i is Sailors, so "$UPP $i" has the value Oh! Sailors, which becomes the new
value of UPP, and so on.

23.5.2 Internal command continue
This command causes the structure to move to the next iteration of
the **for** or **while** loop in which it appears. We "jump" to the **done** of
the loop. We will take the **classify** procedure again, replacing the
break with **continue**.

```
for i
. . .
[0-9]*) continue ;;
*);;
esac
done
echo . . .
```

Now, **classify** ignores the arguments starting with a number. When
a number is encountered (pattern [0-9]*), the structure moves on the
done of the **for** loop, which continues normally:

```
$ classify Oh! how many Sailors, 8, how many Captains 3
how many how many
Oh! Sailors, Captains
$
```

23.5.3 Rerouting on events
First we need to explain the concept of an event. We can see this in
the following procedure **trapex**:

```
echo victor > /tmp/prov$$
echo temporary file created, I sleep for 5 seconds
sleep 5
echo wake up!
rm /tmp/prov$$
```

Executed normally, this procedure is of no interest. It creates a
temporary file, goes to sleep for 5 seconds, and on awakening destroys the temporary file. We terminate it by pressing the DEL key
(the key that interrupts a command, 1.9), but after receiving its
message 'temporary file created...'.

```
$ trapex
temporary file created, I sleep for 5 seconds    = go ahead
                                                 = you regain
                                                 = control
$
```

Instead of waiting the full 5 seconds **trapex** was interrupted when
you pressed DEL, and everything appears normal. When you pressed the
DEL key, you caused an event. Everything happens as though when it
received the DEL message, the trap procedure was executing the
internal command **exit**; and that is just what happens. If DEL had

been pressed before the reawakening message, the temporary file
/tmp/prov$$ would still exist.

We say that **trapex** has been rerouted on receipt of the DEL.

We also say that a signal has been sent to the **trapex** process.
There are several possible signals in UNIX, each having a name and a
number (from 1 to 15). We shall only mention the two most useful for
everyday use of the shell language. These are:

SIGINT, number 2, sent when DEL is keyed.
SIGTERM, number 15, which is produced when you kill a process
initiated in the background, using the **kill** command.

Mastering the event: the internal command **trap**

It often happens that a procedure creates temporary files for its
own use which are destroyed at the end of the procedure. When such a
procedure is interrupted by DEL, how are these temporary files
destroyed?

The **trap** command allows one to specify a list of commands to be
executed on receipt of certain signals, all within a procedure.

We shall limit our use of **trap** to the use of signals 2 and 15,
that is, for abandoning the procedure.

If we alter **trapex** thus:

```
trap 'echo Here is the signal! rm -f /tmp/prov$$ ; exit ' 2
echo victor > /tmp/prov$$
echo temporary file created, I sleep for 5 seconds
sleep 5
echo wake up!
rm /tmp/prov$$
```

We now execute **trapex** as before. We wait for the creation message
and then press DEL:

```
$ trapex                                        = gives
temporary file created, I sleep for 5 seconds   = press CTRL-C
Here is the signal!
$ ls /tmp/prov*                                 = does this exist?
/tmp/prov* not found
$
```

On receiving signal 2, the command list mentioned between single
quotes after **trap** has been executed, and in particular the temporary
files have been destroyed.

Here only signal 2 has been trapped in this way. To trap signal 15 too, we should have to write:

```
trap 'rm -f /tmp/prov$$  ;exit'    2 15
```

Now, on receipt of 2 or 15, **trapex** would have been rerouted to execute:

```
rm -f /tmp/prov$$   ; exit
```

(Option **-f** causes the file to be destroyed, without hesitation or message; which is what we wanted here.)

Note that **trap** must appear before the creation of temporary fil- es. Without **trap,** the default processing applies, that is, a simple **exit.**

The list of commands after the **trap** can consist of any commands. If you want to abandon the procedure, you should include **exit,** but it is not obligatory. In its absence, after the rerouting, the procedure will start again where it was interrupted.

Finally, several traps can appear in the same procedure, altering as it progresses what it has to do on receipt of the signals we have mentioned.

Traps are valid for the procedure in which they are defined and for the processes called by this procedure.

23.6 Summary

Every process sends a return code to the shell at the end of its execution.

This code is:

accessible by **$?** (special variable)

used by the control structures if-then-else, while and until loops, which test the return code of the last command in the command-list.

exit [n]

terminates the procedure with return code n; if this is ab- sent, with the return code of the last command executed.

if then else structure

        if command-list-1
        then command-list-2
        fi

```
if command-list-1
then command-list-2
else command-list-3
fi
```

The **then** branch is executed if the return code of the last command in command-list-1 is zero. If not, the **else** branch is executed, if there is one.

while loop

```
while command-list-1
do
command-list-2
done
```

For as long as the return code of the last command in command-list1 is zero, command-list-2 is executed.

until loop

```
until command-list-1
do
command-list-2
done
```

As long as the return code of the last command in command-list-1 is zero, command-list-2 is executed.

trap commands 2 15

on receiving the signal 2 or 15, the specified commands are executed.

24 vi — a display oriented interactive text editor

24.0 Session aim

Earlier in the book, we met the line-oriented editors **ed** and **ex**. We chose to concentrate on **ex**, as it forms the basis for a visual editor, **vi**, which originated with Berkeley UNIX 4.2.

All of the **ex** commands can be used with **vi**, which we now look at in greater detail.

When using **vi**, the screen of your terminal acts as a window into the file being edited. If your screen has 24 lines and 80 columns, **vi** will display a 23 by 80 section of your file - the bottom line of the screen is used to input **ex** commands and for information (e.g. error messages!) from **vi**. You can move backwards and forwards in the file; **vi** will display the section that you are currently working on.

It is also possible to move the cursor backwards and forwards about the screen in units of characters, words, sentences and paragraphs. You can combine these movement operations with a small set of commands (such as delete and change).

vi has to know the terminal characteristics for your terminal; that is, how to move the cursor for any particular make or type of terminal. This information is stored in a file called **/etc/termcap.** If your terminal cannot run **vi** (you can find out by trying to run **vi**; if it does not know your terminal type, it will run **ex** instead), ask your system manager to add an entry for your terminal in the **termcap** file. Once this is done, you should be able to use **vi**.

We can now think of **ex** as a version of **vi** which uses a one-line window on the file being edited.

As **vi** is a display-oriented editor, it is hard to give full examples of its capabilities on the printed page; we recommend that you use **vi** and experiment with its capabilities. Once mastered, however, you will find it difficult to return to line-oriented editors. Be warned!

24.1 States of operation

vi has three states/modes:

a) command state: **vi** receives and interprets commands from the keyboard. This state is the normal (and initial) state of **vi**. The escape character <escape> will cancel partial commands.

b) insert state: arbitrary text can be entered, terminated by <escape> to return to command state.

c) last line state: when you type :, /, ?, or !, **vi** moves the cursor to the bottom of the screen. Here, following the : character, we can enter **ex** commands. Input is terminated with a <return> to execute the command or <esc> to cancel. The ! character should be followed by a shell command (as in **ex**).

It is (very) possible to forget what state you are currently in; just hit <escape> a few times until the terminal beeps. At this point you will be back in command mode.

24.2 Entering and leaving vi

$ vi filename

where **filename** is the name of the file to be edited or created. **vi** displays the first window from the file, and on the last line of the screen outputs the number of lines and characters that it contains (as does **ex**).

If the file has fewer lines than the screen, every line past the end of the file is blank, except for a tilde (~) in the first character position.

While editing proceeds, all the changes are made to a copy of the file held in the editor's buffer. To write out these modifications and leave (or quit) the editor, we can type **ZZ** while in command mode. Or, we could type

:wq

The colon places us in "last line" state, and we can then type the two **ex** commands we have met before, **write** and **quit**.

If we decide that we do not want to make the changes, we can abandon the session, leaving the original file unchanged, by typing

:q!<return>

24.3 Movements

24.3.1 Cursor movements
In order to give some examples, let us postulate a tiny window on

the file as shown below:


```
    1 2 3 4 5 6 7 8

 1 ┌t h e   c a t─┐
 2 │s a t   o n   │
 3 │t h e   m a t │        <- last line
 4 │              │
   └──────────────┘
```

We can then describe the following cursor movements:

H (home)   – move cursor to top left corner of window
M (middle) – move cursor to start of middle line of window
L (last)   – move cursor to last line of text of window

In our ·simple example, **H** would move us to position (1,1) – the character 't' in the word 'the' on line 1. **M** would move us to position (1,2) – the character 's' in the word 'sat' on line 2. **L** would move us to position (1,3) – the character 't' in the word 'the' on line 3. By moving, we mean the cursor would move to the specified position and flash there. We indicate this in the following examples by showing the letter covered by the cursor in **bold**.

We can also move on a per-character basis. To move right, we type **^L** or the right point arrow character (if our keyboard has one).

        t**h**e cat
becomes
        th**e** cat

To move left, we type **^H** or the left pointing arrow character.

        the ca**t**
becomes
        the c**a**t

To move up, we type **^K** or the upward arrow character.

        the cat
        s**a**t on
becomes
        t**h**e cat
        sat on

To move down, we type ^J or the downward arrow character.

        the cat
        sat on
becomes
        the cat
        sat on

The <return> character will move the cursor to the start of the
next line.

        the cat
        sat on
becomes
        the cat
        sat on

The commands that we have seen so far move the cursor in terms of
character positions on the screen. We can also move the cursor in
terms of words.
    w (or **W**) moves the cursor to the beginning of the next word in
the text.

        the cat
becomes
        the cat

    b (or **B**) moves to the beginning of the previous word. If the
cursor is already in a word, it moves to the beginning of that word.

        the cat
becomes
        the cat
becomes
        the cat

    e (or **E**) moves to the end of the next word.

        the cat
becomes
        the cat
becomes
        the cat

Note that **W**, **B** and **E** ignore punctuation marks; such marks are not considered to be part of words.

24.4 Window movements

We can move through the file by moving our window. If we have finished with the current window, we can move to the next by typing ^F; we can go back to the previous window by typing ^B. We can also move in terms of half-windows; ^D will show us the bottom half of the current window and the top half of the next window, while ^U will show the bottom half of the previous window and the top half of the current window. The results of ^D and ^U become our current window.

So we can move backwards and forwards through the file in terms of windows and half-windows, as we please. Such movement is referred to as scrolling.

If we want to see a specific line, we can move both the window and cursor to the line by typing n**G** where n is the number of the line. We could also issue the **ex** command

:n<return>

24.5 Search commands

Just as in **ex**, we give the strings that we are searching for in the delimiters // for forward search, and ?? for backward search.

Notice that when you type / or ?, **vi** enters "last line" state and moves the cursor to the bottom of the screen. You then type the string that you are looking for. You do not need to type a closing delimiter; <return> will do (i.e. /**cat**<return>).

If **vi** can find the string, it will position the cursor at the start of the next occurrence of the string. If the string is not in the current window, **vi** will move to the appropriate window.

24.6 Insertion and deletion

To insert text, you must first position the cursor (as shown above) at the character position that you wish to insert text from. Note that this position can be anywhere in the text, and anywhere on a line; it does not have to be the first character position. Once the cursor is in position, you can type **i** to enter insert mode. From this point on, **vi** leaves command mode and enters insert mode; any characters that you type become part of the text, until you type the <escape> key.

The **i** command inserts text to the left of the current cursor position. On some terminals it may appear that you are overtyping existing text; don't worry! This text will reappear when you type

<escape>. Some terminals will move the characters on the screen to the right as you insert text; try setting the "redraw" option by typing

:set redraw<return>

when you start the **vi** session.

     the **c**at sat on the mat
type **i** and 'g' --
     the g**c**at sat on the mat
and 'o' --
     the go**c**at sat on the mat
and 'o' --
     the goo**c**at sat on the mat
and 'd' --
     the good**c**at sat on the mat
and ' ' --
     the good **c**at sat on the mat
and <escape>
     the good **c**at sat on the mat

You can also use the **a** command, which inserts text to the right of the current cursor position.

It is possible to delete characters, words and lines. While in command mode, every **x** that you type will delete the character at the current cursor position. To delete a word, **dw** will remove the next word in the line, from the current cursor position.

     which **w**ord will it delete,
becomes
     which **w**ill it delete,
becomes
     which **i**t delete.

To delete a line, type **dd** and the line that the cursor is currently on will be deleted.

We can also change words by typing **cw**; this places a $ symbol at the end of the word that we are changing. This places us in insert mode; we can type as many characters as we like, ending with the <escape> character.

     the **g**ood cat sat on the mat
type **cw** --
     the **g**oo$ cat sat on the mat

```
type 'n' --
      the noo$ cat sat on the mat
type 'a' --
      the nao$ cat sat on the mat
type 's' --
      the nas$ cat sat on the mat
type 't' --
      the nast cat sat on the mat
                 -
type 'y' --
      the nasty cat sat on the mat
                  -
type <escape>
```

It is possible to repeat commands a number of times by prefixing
them with a number. For example, **5dw** will delete the next five
words. Similarly, **10x** will delete the next ten characters.

24.7 Summary of vi

This section contains a summary of **vi** commands. We recommend trial-
and-error practice in order to learn and master **vi**. It is a powerful
editor, and your work will be amply rewarded! (Our thanks are due to
I.M. Guffick and E.S. Garnett of the Department of Computing,
University of Lancaster, for some of the material used in this
chapter.)

The following is a brief description of the more commonly used **vi**
commands. Remember that the notation **^K** means that the control key
and the K key must be depressed together.

24.7.1 Cursor movement commands

Home (**H**)
Move cursor to start of top line of window.

Middle (**M**)
Move cursor to middle line of window.

Last (**L**)
Move cursor to last line of window.

Move Right (**^L** or ->)
Move cursor right.

Move left (**^H** or <-)
Move cursor left.

Move Up (^K or ^)
Move cursor up to previous line.

Return (^M or <return>)
Move cursor to the start of the next line.

w (or **W**)
Advance cursor to beginning of next word in the line.

b (or **B**)
Retreat to beginning of the previous word in the line.

e (or **E**)
Advance to end of the next word in the line.

+
Move cursor to first non-space, tab, or newline character on the next line.

-
Move cursor to first non-space, tab, or newline character on the previous line.

Note: **W,B** and **E** ignore punctuation.

24.7.2 Window movement commands

Previous page (^B)
Move back one window

Window Down (^D)
Scroll down 1/2 window.

Window Up (^U)
Scroll up 1/2 window.

Go to (n**G**)
Move window and cursor to line n of file.
   G
   Move window and cursor to last line of file.

24.7.3 Search commands

Forward Search (/)

Search forward for the next occurrence of **string,** and then move cursor to it.

Reverse Search (**?**)
Search back for the next occurrence of **string,** and then move cursor to it.

Line Beginning (**∧**)
Search for line beginning with **string,** e.g. **?∧string**

Line Ending (**$**)
Search for line ending with **string,** e.g. **/string$**

Note: **/** and **?** are last line commands.

24.7.4 Reorganising text commands

Yank (**y**)
When preceded by any name a–z will yank (pick up) the object following it into named buffer.

Put (**p**)
When preceded by a name puts contents of buffer after or below the cursor.
   P
      Puts contents before or above the cursor.

Yank Line (**yy**)
Pick up line.
   n**yy**
      Pick up n lines.

Put Line : **p** (or **P**)
Put lines after (before) cursor.

Note: to distinguish between buffer names and the abbreviated command set prefix the buffer name by the escape character '"'. For example, "a5yy picks up 5 lines in buffer 'a'.
   "ap puts contents of buffer 'a' after the cursor.

24.7.5 Insertion and deletion commands

To insert text,

(i)   Position cursor.

(ii) Type **i** to enter insert mode.

(iii) Type in characters, terminating with <esc>.

(On some dumb terminals it may appear that existing text is being undesirably overwritten; it in fact reappears when the <esc> key is pressed.)

Insert (**i**)
Insert text to the left of the current cursor position.

Append (**a**)
Include text to the right of the current cursor position.
   A
      Append text to end of current line.

Clear Line (**o**)
Add a clear line after current line.
   O
      Add a clear line before current line.

Delete Line (**dd**)
Delete current line. (A @ character may appear in place of the line. Type ΔR to redraw the window.)
   n**dd**
      Delete n lines.

Delete Character (**x**)
Delete character at current cursor position.
   n**x**
      Delete n number of characters from the current cursor position.

Replace Character (**r**)
Replace character at current cursor position.

Delete Word (**dw**)
Delete a word forwards.

Undo (**u**)
Undo last single change.
U
Undo all changes to current line.

25 Supplementary details

25.0 Session aim

This miscellaneous session will amplify and complete various topics tackled or touched upon during the preceding sessions, which were not central to the main discussion at the time.

25.1 Achieving precision

In the event of error in a shell procedure, the procedure is usually abandoned. Here we are thinking of errors that relate to programming in the shell language, not errors that exist in a 'pure' program that may be called in a procedure.

The simplest technique is to call the incorrect procedure thus:

```
$ sh -v proced
```

where **proced** is the name of the procedure, and **v** means verbose! This cause the lines of the procedure to be listed as they are read. This should help you to discover the error.

The following points will facilitate shell programming:

a) verify the number of arguments passed
b) test the return codes (**$?**) of the the 'key' processes that the procedure calls
c) beware of non-existent files
d) in case of error or any anomalies (wrong number of arguments, for example), always abandon the procedure by **exit 1** (or **exit 2**, etc; remember, **exit 0** means that all is well). If you include this procedure in another later, you will be able to test its return code usefully.
e) do not write in a dense style; the shell language can quickly become unreadable if you do not take care. Use intermediate variables, or recopy certain positional variables into variables with an explanatory name; this can be useful a few months later when **$2**, **$3**, etc no longer mean very much to you.

25.2 Internal command : (colon)

It would be incorrect to say that this command does nothing. In fact, it evaluates any arguments and sends a zero return code. It allows you to insert comments in a procedure, for example; it also serves to create 'infinite' loops.

```
: infinite while loop                   = note the space after colon
while :
do
echo for ever
done
```

   If you try this, remember to stop it with CTRL-C!

25.3 .profile file

In your home directory there is a file called **.profile** (note period). For example:

```
$ cd /users/moira                       = home directory
$ ls -a                                 = gives
.                                       = the directory itself
..                                      = the parent directory
.profile

etc ...
$
```

   This file is a shell procedure, executed automatically at the login stage.

   It contains various initialisations (of the terminal, for example), generally done by the system supervisor. The **.profile** file is also where certain special shell variables are initialised. Berkeley 4.2 UNIX also has a number of other special . files, such as **.login, .cshrc**, etc. Check your system.

25.4 Reserved variables

Several shell variables are reserved, because they are used by the shell or its utilities. They are normally defined in your **.profile.**

25.4.1 PS1 and PS2 variables

PS1 contains the main call character, by default, which is the dollar **$. PS1** can be changed by the user, to be included for example in his **.profile** file.

```
PS1='%'
```

The same applies to **PS2**, which contains the secondary call character, namely > by default.

25.4.2 HOME variable
This contains the name of your home directory, for example:

```
$ echo $HOME                            = gives
/users/moira
$
```

$HOME is the default argument of the command **cd:**

```
$ pwd
/users/moira/juliette/corresp
$ cd
$ pwd
/users/moira
$
```

24.4.3 IFS variable
When we were studying how to analyse a command line (see 19.1, 21.1
and 21.5.19), the main delimiting character mentioned was the space
character. But in fact, there are three principle delimiters: the
space, the new-line and the tab character.
    The **IFS** variable contains all of these. This variable can be al-
tered (temporarily, for example for the life of a procedure), which
can sometimes facilitate string handling or division into positional
variables (by **set**).

25.4.4 PATH variable, execution directory
In session 16 we said that we should remain in the same directory to
create and execute our sample procedures. In fact, we should normally specify a complete file name to the shell for it to execute. (A
complete name begins with a slash, and 'passes' through all
intermediate directories.) For example:

```
$ /usr/bin/expr 3 + 23
```

    If the command name is incomplete, as in

```
$ mydate
```

the shell searches for the **mydate** file in the current directory.
Hence the advice to remain there.

However, **expr,** as above, is not in our current directory, and the majority of the commands that we have used (**ls, cat,** etc) are not either. Nonetheless, we have never used a complete name.

In fact, where a name is incomplete, the shell goes through several directories until it finds the requested file. The names of these directories are held in a reserved shell variable, called **PATH.** For example

```
$ echo $PATH                    = will produce something like
/bin:/usr/bin
$
```

The colons separate the directories where executable files are to be found. With **PATH,** whenever the command name is incomplete, the shell will go through the directories in the following order:

1) the current directory
2) **/bin**
3) **/usr/bin**

if nothing is found, an error message appears.

This **PATH** variable is initialised in the **.profile** file. It can be altered, for example, by adding a directory name (with colons).

In this way, you can create your own set of commands and execute them from any of your directories.

For everyday use, there is no need to be concerned with other reserved variables, such as **TERM** (type of terminal), **MAIL** (electronic mail), etc.

25.5 Exported variables
We know that the shell variables are only recognised within the procedure in which they appear.

This is inconvenient for variables like **PATH, TERM** and **MAIL,** which must be recognised by all processes. The internal command **export** allows the difficulty to be overcome. In your **.profile,** there will doubtless be a line like:

```
export PATH MAIL TERM
```

This means that these variables are exported; any process has access to them.

25.6 Further investigation
If you consult other manuals and more advanced books on UNIX, you

will see many more possibilities for using the shell that we have been unable to examine in this book. For example, the **for** and **while** loop structures can be considered to be processes, and as such have their input/outputs redirected; or again, a shell procedure can call itself (recursion).

25.7 Summary

sh -v proced

> execution of **proced** with listing of lines as they are read by the shell.

:

> internal command which evaluates its arguments and sends a zero return code (true)

export

> the shell variables mentioned are exported; they are then recognised by all processes (local variables become global)

Reserved variables

PS1

> primary call character (**$** default)

PS2

> secondary call character (> default)

HOME

> user's home directory

IFS

> set of delimiters used for the analysis of a string (by default, space, tab and new-line)

PATH

> set of directories in which the specified command is searched for. (The two standard directories are: **/bin** and **/usr/bin.**)

Epilogue

Have we achieved our aim? This was to examine the main utilities of UNIX, highlight the essential characteristics of the shell, convey an impression of all its possibilities, and above all enable you to get one foot in the stirrup. We hope to have convinced you that, with a minimum of knowledge, it is possible to achieve much with the shell: using it often avoids the need to program (better programming is less programming) and, where programming is necessary, you will be encouraged to program in the UNIX style.

UNIX is often criticised for being unapproachable. We think that this is spurious. UNIX is first of all a framework in which to work, not a 'definitive' system; this makes it able to evolve without much difficulty and to offer more attractive man/machine interfaces than the originals, such as windows and mice.

Furthermore, one should beware of superficial friendliness, which can be the source of great inconvenience when you want to combine programs, exchange data between them, or play (in every sense of the word) with the available tools.

Between the repetitive use of push-button software and the absurd (re)development of software already in existence, there is room for the measured intervention of the user who wants to take the tools made available to him and adapt and combine them for his precise needs.

Appendix 1 Internal commands

Internal commands are those commands internal to the shell. In contrast to the general case, they do not require a disk to be searched for an executable file, and are therefore appreciably faster. For this reason, the recent versions of UNIX tend to have as internal those commands that are frequently used in procedures, commands like **echo, test, expr**, etc, that were originally external.

The following list is restricted to those commands and options discussed in this book. Items between square brackets are optional.

:

> this does nothing, or almost; it evaluates its arguments and sends a zero (true) return code.

break

> interrupts a **for** or **while** loop.

continue

> interrupts the current iteration of a **for** or **while** loop and moves to the next loop.

cd [directory]

> change current directory

eval

> evaluates its arguments, then transfers the result to the shell which reads and executes it.

exit [n]

> causes the current shell procedure to stop; the number **n** of the return code can be provided. If **n** is not provided, the return code is that of the last command to be executed.

export [variable]

> variables given as parameters will be recognised by all processes (usually, a shell variable is only recognised within the procedure that creates it).

read [variable]

> reads a line at the standard input of the procedure in which it appears. The successive words of this line are assigned in order to the shell variables mentioned. The remaining words are assigned to the last variable.The return code is zero until the end of the file is reached.

set arguments

> the current arguments are assigned, in order, to **$1**, **$2**, ...
> **$#** and **$*** are also altered. (Previous values are lost.)

sh –v

> the lines read by the shell are printed.

shift

> the positional variables 2,3, ... are shifted. After **shift**, **$1**
> accesses the old **$2**, and so on.
>
> The number of arguments **$#** is decremented by one, and **$*** is
> also updated.

trap 'sequence-of-commands' nl n2 ...

> sequence-of-commands will be executed on receipt of signals
> nl, n2 ... by the shell.

Appendix 2 Special characters and reserved words

This list only contains those that have been discussed in this book.

	pipe symbol
;	command separator
;;	**case** delimiter
&	background command
()	command grouping
<	standard input redirection
<<	input to here document
>	standard output redirection
>>	additional standard output redirection

generic special characters

*	matches any string, including empty string
?	matches any character
[...]	matches one of the characters included

substitution

| $ ... | shell variable substitution |
| '...' | standard output command substitution |

neutralisaton

\	neutralises the following character
'...'	neutralises included characters except the quote
"..."	neutralises included characters except $ ' \ "

reserved words

if then else elif fi

case in esac

for while until do done

Appendix 3 Examples

Here are two examples of shell procedures actually used on our system.

Example 1
The original shell (UNIX V7) cannot repeat the last command executed, unlike the Berkeley UNIX shell. To remedy this, we wrote the following procedure **myrep**, which we illustrate with some examples of its use.

```
$ myrep 3 date
Wed Dec 10 10:36:21 GMT 1986
Wed Dec 10 10:36:22 GMT 1986
Wed Dec 10 10:36:22 GMT 1986
```

The syntax of **myrep** is in fact:

```
myrep n commands
```

where **n** is the repeat factor (positive integer or zero), and **commands** can be a simple command or a list of commands between single quotes.
Here is another fuller example:

```
$ myrep 3 'date; echo ---------   cat - message' > pileon
$ cat pileon
Wed Dec 10 10:36:27 GMT 1986
---------
These are the continuing voyages of the Starship Enterprise;
Its on-going mission ....
Wed Dec 10 10:36:28 GMt 1986
---------
These are the continuing voyages of the Starship Enterprise;
Its on-going mission ....
Wed Dec 10 10:36:29 GMT 1986
---------
```

These are the continuing voyages of the Starship Enterprise;
Its on-going mission ....
$

   The list of commands between single quotes is repeated three
times. Neutralisation is essential. The semi-colon must only be
interpreted within **myrep**; the same applies for the pipe. On the
other hand, redirection of the standard output from **myrep** to **pileon**
must be interpreted from the beginning; the result of the repetition
is redirected (a similar situation to that with multiple
inheritance, see 17.1.1). Do not confuse with:

```
$ myrep 3 'date; echo ---------   cat - message > pileon'
```

here, on each repeat the contents of **pileon** are overwritten. We
should have inserted >> instead of >.
   Here is the listing of **myrep** (each line is numbered):

```
$ cat -n  myrep
    1  case $# in
    2  0 1 ) echo 'usage : rep n command';exit 1;;
    3  esac
    4
    5  case $1 in
    6  -* 0) exit 0;;
    7  *[A-z]:) echo "rep : $1 non numeric";exit 1;;
    8  esac
    9
   10  co=$1
   11  shift
   12
   13  for i in `gnatu 1 $co`
   14  do
   15          eval $*
   16          case $? in
   17          1 2) echo "incident on iteration number $i"; exit 1;;
   18          esac
   19  done
$
```

   We shall comment line by line (number i returns to line i).

1 to 3
        control number of arguments, which cannot be less than 2

(repetition factor and a simple command or one between single quotes).

5 to 8

control first parameter; if negative or zero, initiates leaving **myrep** (6)

if not strictly numerical, quit **myrep** with error message (7).

10

save repetition factor in variable **co**.

11

after **shift**, **$*** only represents what follows the repetition factor.

13

start of repeat loop

gnatu is a program that we wrote in C which generates the sequence of integer numbers that lie between the two arguments that are sent to it, thus

gnatu 1 $co

generates the sequence 1 2 3 ... until the repeat factor is reached; line 13 is therefore evaluated as

for i **in** 1 2 ... n

in which n is the value of the variable **co**.

The **for** loop will then execute n times, and much faster than if a combination of **expr** and **test** were used.

15

the sequence of commands is evaluated, then passed to the shell.

eval (see 21.5.2 and 21.5.3) is essential here to handle a sequence of commands that might be complex (redirection, regrouping, etc).

16 to 18

summary control of the preceding execution by testing the return code; abandonment and message if code is 1 or 2.

19

end of **for** loop and **myrep**.

It should be noted that the non-use of **expr** and **test** to control the repeat is only sensible if the version of UNIX being used does not possess integrated commands in the shell (see appendix 1). The same remark applies to the use of **case** instead of **test**.

Example 2

It can happen that you have a program (procedure or 'pure' program) that only handles a single file at a time. To make it handle several files would make its use or the analysis of its arguments too complicated. What do you do if you want to apply such a program to a whole set of files?

The procedure **map** can help in such cases. Its general form is as follows:

map command fill fil2 ...

where **command,** or bewteen single or double quotes with arguments and/or input/output redirection. fill fil2 ... are the names of files.

Here is the listing of **map:**

```
1  PROC=$1
2  shift
3
4  for j
5  do
6    echo "debugging $PROC on file $j"
7    eval $PROC $j
8  done
```

Here is a line by line commentary:

1

the command is copied into the variable **PROC;** it is assumed that the command is placed within single or double quotes if necessary, in order to make only a single argument.

2

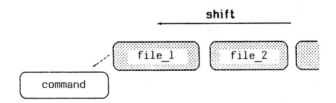

after **shift,** all the remaining arguments are file names.

4 to 7

loop on file names

6

evaluated (by **eval**) as:

file command

which is transmitted to the shell for evaluation and execution.

7

end of **for** loop; end of **map**

Here is an example to illustrate the syntax:

$ map 'proced <' `ls direct`

The procedure **proced** reads at its standard input. Everything happens just as though you had re-entered:

proced <

for each file of the directory **direct.**
We could also have conceived **map** with the help of **sed,** by
inserting in front of each file name the command to be appl-
ied.

Bibliography

Bourne, S.R., The UNIX System,
   Addison-Wesley, 1983.
Bourne, S.R., The UNIX System V Environment,
   Addison-Wesley, 1986.
Brown, P.J., Starting with UNIX,
   Addison-Wesley, 1984.
Christian, K., The UNIX Operating System,
   John Wiley, 1983.
Dunsmuir, M.R.M., and Davies, G.J., Programming the UNIX System,
   Macmillan Education, 1985.
Gautier, R., Using the UNIX System,
   Reston, 1981.
Lomuto, A.N., and Lomuto, N., A UNIX Primer,
   Prentice-Hall, 1983.
McGilton, H., and Morgan, R., Introducing the UNIX System,
   McGraw-Hill, 1983.
Silvester, P.P., The UNIX System Guidebook,
   Springer-Verlag, 1983.
Sobell, M.G., Practical Guide to UNIX System V,
   Addison-Wesley, 1985.
Sobell, M.G., A Practical Guide to the UNIX System,
   Addison-Wesley, 1984.
Thomas, R., and Yates J., A User Guide to the UNIX System,
   McGraw-Hill, 1985.

Index

(Numbering refers to session sections)